JAMESTOWN PUBLISHERS

ENGLISH, YES!

BEGINNING

Learning English Through Literature

BURTON GOODMAN

JAMESTOWN  PUBLISHERS

a division of NTC/CONTEMPORARY PUBLISHING GROUP
Lincolnwood, Illinois USA

Library of Congress Cataloging-in-Publication Data
Goodman, Burton.
    English, yes!: beginning reader/Burton Goodman.
       p. cm.
    ISBN 0-89061-787-2 (alk. paper)
    1. English language–Textbooks for foreign speakers. 2. Readers.
I. Title.
PE1128.G618   1996   95–39825
428.6'4–dc20   CIP

"Crucita" (originally titled "Crucita's Image") © 1987 by
Manuela Williams Crosno. Reprinted by permission
of Manuela Williams Crosno and the author's agent,
Burton Goodman.

Adaptations and/or abridgments are by Burton Goodman.

Editorial Director: Cindy Krejcsi
Executive Editor: Mary Jane Maples
Editor: Michael O'Neill
Design Manager: Ophelia M. Chambliss
Cover and Interior Design: Michael Kelly
Fine Art Illustrations: Adam Young
Production Manager: Margo Goia
Cover Images: Masterfile/© Damir Frkovic
           FPG/© Frank Saragnese 1992

ISBN: 0-89061-787-2

Published by Jamestown Publishers,
a division of NTC/Contemporary Publishing Group, Inc.,
4255 West Touhy Avenue,
Lincolnwood (Chicago), Illinois 60646-1975 U.S.A.
© 1996 Burton Goodman
890 DH 098765

JAMESTOWN PUBLISHERS

ENGLISH, YES!

BEGINNING

CONTENTS

JAMESTOWN PUBLISHERS

ENGLISH, YES!

BEGINNING

WOLF

by Jack London

WOLF

by Jack London

PART 1

This story is about a man, a woman, and a dog. The man's name was Walt. The woman's name was Madge. The dog's name was Wolf.

Madge and Walt were married. They lived in California. They
5   lived in a small house on top of a hill.

One night while Madge and Walt were sleeping, there suddenly was a loud sound. The sound woke them up.

"What was that?" asked Walt.

"I don't know," said Madge. "Let's look outside."

10   They opened the door. They looked around. "Do you see anything?" asked Madge.

"No," said Walt.

Suddenly Madge said, "Look over there!"

On the grass they saw a large, brown dog. The dog looked tired
15   and hungry. It was lost.

Walt and Madge walked toward the dog. The dog **growled** at them. He was not a friendly dog.

"The dog is hungry," said Madge. "Let's give it some bread and milk."

20   They went back to the house and got the food. They put the food on the ground. The dog did not want to eat the food while they were there.

"Let's go back to the house," said Walt.

They went back to the house and looked out the window.

25   The dog began to eat. The dog was **starved**. It ate all the food very quickly.

"That dog eats like a wolf," said Walt.

"It looks like a wolf, too," said Madge. "Let's call him 'Wolf.'"

The next morning they **fed** Wolf again. This time the dog was a
little more friendly. He let them come near him.

In the afternoon their neighbor, Mrs. Johnson, **dropped in**.

She saw Wolf. She said to Madge and Walt, "I didn't know you
had a dog."

"We didn't," said Madge. "We found this dog last night. It was
outside the house."

Mrs. Johnson was surprised. "Where did this dog come from?"
she asked.

"We don't know," said Walt. "It was lost. It came here."

Mrs. Johnson said, "My brother, Skiff, lives in Alaska. I visited
him there last year. This dog looks like the dogs I saw in Alaska. He
looks like the big dogs that pull sleds there."

Madge and Walt looked at each other. They were surprised.
Madge said, "But how could Wolf get here all the way from Alaska?"

YOU CAN ANSWER THESE QUESTIONS

Put an *x* in the box next to the correct answer.

Reading Comprehension

1. Madge and Walt lived in
   - ❏ **a.** California.
   - ❏ **b.** Alaska.
   - ❏ **c.** Texas.

2. Their house was
   - ❏ **a.** on top of a hill.
   - ❏ **b.** on a busy street.
   - ❏ **c.** near some tall trees.

3. Madge and Walt woke up because they heard
   - ❏ **a.** a radio.
   - ❏ **b.** someone calling.
   - ❏ **c.** a loud sound.

4. Madge and Walt saw a large, brown
   - ❏ **a.** wolf.
   - ❏ **b.** dog.
   - ❏ **c.** sled.

5. The dog was
   - ❏ **a.** lost.
   - ❏ **b.** small.
   - ❏ **c.** happy.

6. Mrs. Johnson said that Wolf looked like
   - ❏ **a.** her dog.
   - ❏ **b.** her brother's dog.
   - ❏ **c.** dogs she saw in Alaska.

Vocabulary

7. The dog ate all the food quickly. The dog was starved. The word *starved* means
   - ❏ **a.** very hungry.
   - ❏ **b.** very small.
   - ❏ **c.** very smart.

8. The dog was not friendly. It growled. When it *growled*, it
   - ❏ **a.** smiled.
   - ❏ **b.** made a noise.
   - ❏ **c.** sat down.

9. Madge and Walt fed Wolf again the next morning. The word *fed* means
   - ❏ **a.** yelled at.
   - ❏ **b.** hit.
   - ❏ **c.** gave food to.

Idioms

10. Their neighbor, Mrs. Johnson, dropped in. The idiom *drop in* means
    - ❏ **a.** fell down.
    - ❏ **b.** visited.
    - ❏ **c.** hurt yourself.

How many questions did you answer correctly? Circle your score. Then fill in your score on the Score Chart on page 168.

Number Correct	1	2	3	4	5	6	7	8	9	10
Score	10	20	30	40	50	60	70	80	90	100

Exercise A

Understanding the story. Answer each question by writing a complete sentence. Begin each sentence with a capital letter. End each sentence with a period. You may use the line numbers in parentheses to find the answers. The first sentence has been done for you.

1. What was the man's name? (2)

   The man's name was Walt.

2. What was the woman's name? (2)

   _____

3. What was the dog's name? (3)

   _____

4. Where did Madge and Walt live? (4)

   _____

5. What woke up Madge and Walt? (7)

   _____

6. What did they see on the grass? (14)

   _____

7. What did they give the dog? (18)

   _____

8. How much food did the dog eat? (25)

   _____

9. Where did Mrs. Johnson's brother live? (39)

   _____

10. When did Mrs. Johnson visit her brother? (40)

   _____

Exercise B

Building sentences. Make sentences by adding the correct letter. The first sentence has been done for you.

1. _b_ Madge and Walt   **a.** in California.
2. ____ They lived   **b.** were married.
3. ____ A loud sound   **c.** toward the dog.
4. ____ They walked   **d.** woke them up.

Now write the sentences on the lines below. Remember to begin each sentence with a capital letter and to end each sentence with a period.

1. _____

2. _____

3. _____

4. _____

Now do questions 5–8 the same way.

5. ____ The dog   **a.** some bread and milk.
6. ____ They gave it   **b.** fed Wolf again.
7. ____ Madge and Walt   **c.** was not friendly.
8. ____ The next morning they   **d.** looked out the window.

5. _____

6. _____

7. _____

_____

8. _____

_____

Exercise C

Adding vocabulary. On the left are 8 words from the story. Complete each sentence by adding the correct word.

dog

sleds

neighbor

door

married

night

ground

food

1. Madge and Walt were _____.

2. They woke up during the _____.

3. They opened the _____.

4. On the grass they saw a _____.

5. They put some food on the _____.

6. The dog did not eat the _____.

7. Mrs. Johnson was their _____.

8. In Alaska dogs pull _____.

Exercise D

Using verbs correctly. Fill in each blank using the **present tense** of the verb *to be (am, are, is).*

This story _____ about a man, a woman, and a
                    1

dog. The man and the woman _____ married.
                                      2

They live in a small house. It _____ on top of
                                        3

a hill.

One night they hear a loud sound. They _____ surprised.
                                                      4

"What _____ that?" asks the man.
              5

"I _____ not sure," says the woman.
          6

They see a dog. It _____ hungry and tired.
                            7

Changing statements to questions. Change each statement to a question that begins with *Was* or *Were*. Put a question mark at the end of each question. The first one has been done for you.

1. The dog was tired.

Was the dog tired?

2. The dog was hungry.

_____

3. The dog was lost.

_____

4. The dog was outside the house.

_____

5. Madge and Walt were married.

_____

6. The dog was a little more friendly.

_____

7. Madge and Walt were sleeping.

_____

8. Mrs. Johnson was surprised.

_____

9. Mrs. Johnson's brother was in Alaska.

_____

10. Madge and Walt were surprised, too.

_____

Vocabulary review. Write a complete sentence for each word or group of words.

1. married _____

_____

2. sled _____

_____

3. neighbor _____

_____

4. starved _____

_____

5. growled _____

_____

6. fed _____

_____

7. dropped in _____

_____

SHARING WITH OTHERS

It is fun to share ideas with others. Discuss these questions with your partner or with the group. Write your answer to one of the questions.

◆ Which do you like better—dogs or cats? Why?
◆ Why do people like to have pets?
◆ What are some of the problems of having a pet?

_____

_____

_____

_____

PART 2

Madge and Walt fed Wolf every day. They **took long walks** with him. They liked to play with Wolf. Wolf still was not too friendly.

One afternoon Madge came out of the house. She walked down the steps and looked around. She saw Walt. He had a hammer in his hand. He was fixing the fence.

"Where is Wolf?" she asked.

"I don't know," Walt answered. "He was here a minute ago. Maybe he ran after a rabbit."

"I don't see him now," said Madge. "Here, Wolf," she called.

They walked down the road and through the tall grass.

"There he is!" said Walt. He pointed ahead.

Wolf was sitting on top of a large rock. The dog was watching them.

"Good dog," shouted Walt. "Come here."

The dog opened his mouth. He looked at Madge and Walt and ran toward them. He stopped about twenty feet away.

Madge and Walt continued to walk. Wolf ran into the tall grass. Soon they did not see him.

"Wolf will **catch up** with us later," said Madge.

Suddenly they heard something. The sound was coming from the woods. They saw a man. He came out of the woods and walked toward them.

Madge and Walt did not know the man. He was very tall, and he looked very strong. He had wide shoulders. He had long hair and a thick, black beard. He was holding his hat in his hand.

"Good afternoon," said Walt. "Today is a very warm day."

"Yes," said the man. "It's very warm. I'm not used to warm weather. I like cold weather."

Madge smiled. She said, "It's never cold here."

30   "No," said the man. He took a red **handkerchief** out of his pocket and wiped his face with it.

        The man said, "I'm looking for my sister. Her name is Pat Johnson. She lives somewhere around here."

        Madge said, "You must be her brother from Alaska."

35   "Yes," said the man. "My name is Skiff Miller. This visit is a surprise. My sister doesn't know I'm here."

        "She lives nearby," said Walt. "Do you see that big tree over there? There's a little **path** near the tree. Walk up the path. Her house is the first one on the right."

40   "Thank you," Miller said.

        The man started to leave. Madge said, "We'd like to visit you while you're here. We'd like to hear about Alaska."

        Walt said, "Maybe you can have dinner with us some day."

        "Thanks again," Skiff Miller said. "But I will be here for just one

45 day. I'm leaving tomorrow. I have important business in Alaska."

        Just then Wolf ran across the grass. Miller stared at the dog. He kept staring.

        "I don't believe it," he said softly.

Put an *x* in the box next to the correct answer.

Reading Comprehension

1. What was Walt fixing?
   - ❑ **a.** a fence
   - ❑ **b.** a door
   - ❑ **c.** a window

2. Walt thought that Wolf ran after
   - ❑ **a.** a man.
   - ❑ **b.** a rabbit.
   - ❑ **c.** another dog.

3. Skiff Miller was very
   - ❑ **a.** short.
   - ❑ **b.** tall.
   - ❑ **c.** thin.

4. What color was Miller's beard?
   - ❑ **a.** red
   - ❑ **b.** black
   - ❑ **c.** brown

5. Miller liked
   - ❑ **a.** warm weather.
   - ❑ **b.** hot weather.
   - ❑ **c.** cold weather.

6. Miller was staying for
   - ❑ **a.** one day.
   - ❑ **b.** five days.
   - ❑ **c.** two weeks.

Vocabulary

7. Miller took a handkerchief out of his pocket and wiped his face with it. What is a *handkerchief*?
   - ❑ **a.** a piece of cloth
   - ❑ **b.** a piece of wood
   - ❑ **c.** a paper bag

8. Walt told Miller to walk up the path. A *path* is a
   - ❑ **a.** rock.
   - ❑ **b.** house.
   - ❑ **c.** road.

Idioms

9. Madge and Walt took long walks with Wolf. The idiom *take a walk* means
   - ❑ **a.** look for a place to walk.
   - ❑ **b.** go for a walk.
   - ❑ **c.** to be tired from walking.

10. Madge said that Wolf would catch up with them later. When you *catch up* with someone, you
    - ❑ **a.** make fun of someone.
    - ❑ **b.** play a game with someone.
    - ❑ **c.** meet someone.

How many questions did you answer correctly? Circle your score. Then fill in your score on the Score Chart on page 168.

Number Correct	1	2	3	4	5	6	7	8	9	10
Score	10	20	30	40	50	60	70	80	90	100

EXERCISES TO HELP YOU

Exercise A

Understanding the story. Answer each question by writing a complete sentence. Begin each sentence with a capital letter. End each sentence with a period. You may use the line numbers in parentheses to find the answers.

1. How often did Madge and Walt feed Wolf? (1)

   _____

2. What did Walt have in his hand? (4)

   _____

3. What was Walt fixing? (5)

   _____

4. What was Miller holding in his hand? (25)

   _____

5. What did Miller take out of his pocket? (30)

   _____

   _____

6. What did Miller do with the handkerchief? (31)

   _____

   _____

7. Who was Miller looking for? (32)

   _____

8. Why was Miller staying for just one day? (45)

   _____

Exercise B

Building sentences. Make sentences by adding the correct letter.

1. ____ Madge and Walt took	**a.** on top of a large rock.
2. ____ Wolf was sitting	**b.** very strong.
3. ____ The man came out of	**c.** long walks with Wolf.
4. ____ They thought that Skiff Miller was	**d.** the woods.

Now write the sentences on the lines below. Remember to begin each sentence with a capital letter and to end each sentence with a period.

1. _____

2. _____

3. _____

4. _____

_____

Now do questions 5–8 the same way.

5. ____ Madge and Walt did not know	**a.** at the dog.
6. ____ Skiff Miller was holding his hat	**b.** the man.
7. ____ Walt pointed to a path	**c.** near a tree.
8. ____ Miller kept staring	**d.** in his hand.

5. _____

6. _____

_____

7. _____

8. _____

Exercise C

Adding vocabulary. On the left are 6 words from the story. Complete each sentence by adding the correct word.

nearby   **1.** The dog opened his _____ .

mouth   **2.** Skiff Miller's _____ were wide.

hammer   **3.** Their neighbor, Mrs. Johnson, lived _____ .

shoulders   **4.** Walt used a _____ to fix the fence.

dinner   **5.** Madge and Walt _____ to walk.

continued   **6.** They asked Mr. Miller to have _____ with them.

Exercise D

Part A

Using verbs correctly. Fill in each blank using the **present tense** of the verb *to have (have, has).*

1. Skiff Miller _____ wide shoulders.

2. He _____ long hair.

3. He also _____ a beard.

4. Walt told Miller, "Maybe you can _____ dinner with us."

5. Miller said, "I _____ important business in Alaska."

Part B

Now fill in each blank using the **past tense** of the verb *to be (was, were)*.

1. Walt said, "Wolf _____ here a minute ago."

2. The dog _____ not very friendly.

3. Madge and Walt _____ very surprised.

4. The man _____ very tall.

5. He _____ very strong.

6. His sister _____ their neighbor.

7. They _____ sorry he could not stay for dinner.

Exercise E

Adding an adjective. Complete the sentences below by writing the correct adjective. Each sentence tells something about the story. Use each adjective once.

      tall   **warm**   **black**   **large**   **important**

1. Miller did not wear a hat because it was a very _____ day.

2. They could not see the dog because he ran into the _____ grass.

3. Skiff Miller had _____ business in Alaska.

4. The man had long hair and a thick, _____ beard.

5. The dog sat on a _____ rock.

Exercise F

Vocabulary review. Write a complete sentence for each word or group of words.

1. nearby _____

   _____

2. shoulders _____

   _____

3. continued _____

   _____

4. handkerchief _____

   _____

5. path _____

   _____

6. take a walk _____

   _____

7. catch up _____

   _____

SHARING WITH OTHERS

It is fun to share ideas with others. Discuss these questions with your partner or with the group. Write your answer to one of the questions.

◆ Which do you like better, cold weather or hot weather? Why?
◆ Which season (summer, winter, spring, fall) do you like the most? Why?

_____

_____

_____

_____

_____

PART 3

Skiff Miller sat down on a log. He looked at the dog. Miller shook his head. "I don't believe it," he said again.

Wolf heard Skiff Miller's words. The dog ran to the man and looked at the man's hands. He licked them with his tongue. Miller
5 reached out and patted the dog's head.

Miller looked up at Madge and Walt. "I had to sit down," Miller said. "I was very surprised."

"We're suprised, too," said Walt. "Wolf isn't very friendly. But he was friendly to you."

10 "Is that what you call him—'Wolf'?" asked Skiff.

"Yes," said Madge. "I wonder why he's friendly to you." She thought for a moment. Then she said, "Maybe it's because you're from Alaska. Wolf is from Alaska, too, you know."

"Yes," said Miller. "I know."

15 Miller reached out again and touched one of Wolf's paws. "The dog's paw feels soft," Miller said. "He hasn't pulled a sled for a long time."

"That's true," said Walt.

No one spoke for a moment. Then Madge said, "I'm surprised
20 that Wolf let you touch him."

Skiff Miller stood up suddenly. He said, "How long have you had this dog?"

Before anyone could answer Wolf barked.

Madge and Walt were **shocked**. They never heard Wolf bark
25 before. The dog barked again.

"Wolf never barked before," said Madge.

Miller smiled. "I have heard him bark before," he said.

Madge stared at Miller. "What do you mean?" she said. Suddenly she felt scared. "You just met Wolf."

30 Miller looked closely at Madge. "You're wrong about that," he said. His voice sounded angry. "This is *my* dog.

"Yes," said Miller. "This is my dog! I thought you could see that from the way he acted. He's *my* dog. His name is not 'Wolf.' His name is 'Brown.'"

35 "How do you know he's your dog?" Walt asked loudly.

"He is!" was the answer.

Walt looked at Miller. "You can't **prove** that," said Walt.

Miller said, "The dog is mine. I guess I should know my own dog. This dog is mine. I can prove it! Watch!'

40 Skiff Miller turned to the dog. "Brown!" shouted Miller.

The dog turned around and looked at Miller.

"Turn!" shouted Miller. "Turn! Get ready!"

The dog turned **at once**. It stared ahead and waited.

"He knows my voice," Miller explained. "He listens to me. Turn

45 again!" said Miller. The dog turned again.

Walt looked unhappy.

"He was my best dog," said Miller. "He was the best dog in my team of dogs."

"But you're not going to take him with you?" said Madge.

50 "Yes," said Miller. "I'm taking him back to Alaska."

"To Alaska?" said Walt. "To that cold, cold world? He'll suffer there."

"Yes," said Madge, "Why don't you leave him here? He likes it here! He gets **plenty** of food. And he won't have to pull a sled

55 through the snow."

"He doesn't mind pulling a sled," said Miller. "He's strong, you know."

"But he's happy here," said Walt. "What can you give him in Alaska?"

60 "Work," said Skiff Miller. "I'll give him work. He likes work. And he'll have the cold and the snow. He likes them too. He knows that life. He was born in Alaska. He grew up there."

Skiff Miller shook his head and said, "He may be happy here. But he'll be happier in Alaska."

65 "Well, I won't let you take the dog!" Walt said suddenly. "I don't want to talk about it. The dog is not going!"

YOU CAN ANSWER THESE QUESTIONS

Put an *x* in the box next to the correct answer.

Reading Comprehension

1. The dog
   - ❑ **a.** ran away from Skiff Miller.
   - ❑ **b.** jumped up at Skiff Miller.
   - ❑ **c.** licked Skiff Miller's hands.

2. Skiff Miller said that the dog's paw felt
   - ❑ **a.** soft.
   - ❑ **b.** hard.
   - ❑ **c.** thin.

3. Madge and Walt were surprised that Wolf
   - ❑ **a.** was afraid of Miller.
   - ❑ **b.** was friendly to Miller.
   - ❑ **c.** tried to bite Miller.

4. Miller said that the dog's name was
   - ❑ **a.** Wolf.
   - ❑ **b.** Brown.
   - ❑ **c.** Spot.

5. Miller told Walt and Madge that he would
   - ❑ **a.** leave the dog with them.
   - ❑ **b.** take the dog to Alaska.
   - ❑ **c.** sell the dog to someone.

6. Miller said he would give the dog
   - ❑ **a.** good food.
   - ❑ **b.** a warm house.
   - ❑ **c.** work.

Vocabulary

7. Walt and Madge never heard Wolf bark before. They were shocked. The word *shocked* means
   - ❑ **a.** worried.
   - ❑ **b.** sad.
   - ❑ **c.** surprised.

8. Miller said, "This dog is mine. I can prove it!" When you *prove* something, you
   - ❑ **a.** show that you like it.
   - ❑ **b.** help it.
   - ❑ **c.** show that it is true.

9. Madge said that Wolf got plenty of food. The word *plenty* means
   - ❑ **a.** a little bit.
   - ❑ **b.** a lot.
   - ❑ **c.** the same kind.

Idioms

10. When Miller told the dog to turn, the dog turned at once. The idiom *at once* means
    - ❑ **a.** very soon.
    - ❑ **b.** after a long time.
    - ❑ **c.** after a week.

How many questions did you answer correctly? Circle your score. Then fill in your score on the Score Chart on page 168.

Number Correct	1	2	3	4	5	6	7	8	9	10
Score	10	20	30	40	50	60	70	80	90	100

Exercise A

Understanding the story. Answer each question by writing a complete sentence. Begin each sentence with a capital letter. End each sentence with a period. You may use the line numbers in parentheses to find the answers.

1. What did Skiff Miller sit down on? (1)

   _____

2. Why did Miller sit down? (7)

   _____

3. Where was Skiff Miller from? (13)

   _____

4. How did the dog's paw feel? (16)

   _____

5. Why were Madge and Walt surprised when Wolf barked? (24)

   _____

   _____

6. When Miller shouted "Turn," what did the dog do? (43)

   _____

7. Where was the dog born? (62)

   _____

8. Where did the dog grow up? (62)

   _____

Exercise B

Building sentences. Make sentences by adding the correct letter.

1. _____ Wolf looked	**a.** from Alaska.
2. _____ Skiff Miller reached out and	**b.** at the man's hands.
3. _____ Madge said that the dog was	**c.** the dog bark before.
4. _____ Miller said he had heard	**d.** patted the dog's head.

Now write the sentences on the lines below. Remember to begin each sentence with a capital letter and to end each sentence with a period.

1. _____

2. _____

_____

3. _____

_____

4. _____

Now do questions 5–8 the same way.

5. _____ Madge suddenly	**a.** angry.
6. _____ Skiff Miller's voice sounded	**b.** the dog was strong.
7. _____ The dog stared	**c.** felt scared.
8. _____ Miller said that	**d.** ahead and waited.

5. _____

6. _____

7. _____

8. _____

Exercise C

Adding vocabulary. On the left are 6 words from the story. Complete each sentence by adding the correct word.

tongue   1. Skiff Miller sat down on a _____ .

team   2. The dog _____ the man's hands.

paws   3. He licked the man's hands with his _____ .

log   4. Miller touched one of the dog's _____ .

licked   5. Madge thought the dog would _____ in
               Alaska.

suffer
               6. Brown was the best dog in Miller's _____ of dogs.

Exercise D

Using verbs correctly. Fill in each blank using the **present tense** of the regular verb in parentheses. The first one has been done for you.

1. When he is in Alaska, Brown _____*works*_____ hard. (work)

2. He _____ a sled through the snow. (pull)

3. Brown always _____ to his owner. (listen)

4. When his owner says, "Turn," Brown _____ . (turn)

5. Brown _____ all the time. (bark)

6. He _____ Alaska very much. (like)

The sentences above make a paragraph. Write the paragraph on the lines.

_____

_____

_____

_____

_____

Exercise E

True or false sentences. Write **T** if the sentence is true. Write **F** if the sentence is false.

1. _____ Madge said that Wolf was always friendly to everyone.

2. _____ Skiff Miller was from California.

3. _____ Miller had heard the dog bark before.

4. _____ The dog listened to Miller.

5. _____ Brown was Skiff Miller's best dog.

6. _____ The dog did not like the cold and the snow.

7. _____ The dog grew up in Alaska.

8. _____ Walt said that Miller could take the dog to Alaska.

Exercise F

Vocabulary review. Write a complete sentence for each word or group of words.

1. log _____

_____

2. tongue _____

_____

3. paws _____

_____

4. shocked _____

_____

5. prove _____

_____

6. suffer _____

_____

7. plenty _____

_____

8. team _____

_____

9. licked _____

_____

10. at once _____

_____

SHARING WITH OTHERS

It is fun to share ideas with others. Discuss these questions with your partner or with the group. Write your answer to one of the questions.

◆ What kind of work do you like to do? Why?
◆ What kind of work do you hate (or not like) to do? Why?

_____

_____

_____

_____

_____

_____

_____

_____

PART 4

Miller looked at Walt. "What? What's that?" said Miller. "What's that?"

"I said the dog isn't going with you," said Walt. "I don't believe that he is your dog. Maybe you saw him in Alaska. Maybe he pulled a sled for you once. But you can't prove that he's yours!"

Skiff Miller's mouth opened. But he said nothing. Then his face became red. He was very angry.

Walt said, "The dog listened to you. That's true. But any dog from Alaska would **obey** you. Wolf is probably worth a lot of money. That's why you want him. But you can't prove that he's yours."

"Is that so?" Miller said slowly. He stared down at Walt. Walt was much shorter than Miller. "Well, no one can stop me from taking the dog right now."

Miller raised his **fist** and took a step toward Walt.

Madge stepped between the two men.

"Maybe Mr. Miller is right," she said to Walt. "Wolf does seem to know him. And Wolf did answer to the name of 'Brown.' Wolf was friendly to Mr. Miller **right away**. And Wolf barked—for the first time! Why did he bark? I think I know. Wolf was happy because he found Mr. Miller."

Walt shook his head sadly. Then he said, "I guess you're right, Madge. Wolf isn't really 'Wolf.' His real name is 'Brown.' I guess that he is Mr. Miller's dog."

Madge turned to Skiff Miller. "Would you sell the dog to us?" she asked. "We'd like to buy him."

Miller shook his head. "I'm sorry," he said. His voice was kind. "I had a team of five dogs. Brown was the leader. He was the best dog I ever had."

Miller spoke softly. "I like that dog a lot," he said. "I care about him. When he was **stolen**, I felt sick. I have been looking for him for three years. When I saw him here, I thought I was dreaming. I was so happy. I can't sell this dog to you."

Madge suddenly said, "You say you care about the dog. But you don't!"

Skiff Miller looked surprised. He said, "What do you mean?"

"You say you care about the dog," Madge said. "Then let the dog choose where he wants to live. Maybe he wants to stay here in California. Maybe he likes California better than Alaska."

Skiff Miller said nothing.

"You say you care about the dog," said Madge. "Then do whatever makes him happy."

Miller thought about this. Then he said, "Brown was a good worker. He worked hard. He was never lazy. He's smart, too. He understands you when you talk to him. Look at him now. He knows that we're talking about him."

The dog was lying at Skiff Miller's feet. The dog's ears were standing straight up. The dog looked at Miller. Then he looked at Madge. He watched them when they spoke. He seemed to be listening.

"Yes, he worked hard," said Miller. "And I do like him."

Miller thought about this some more. Then he said to Madge, "The dog has earned the right to choose. I'll do whatever he wants."

YOU CAN ANSWER THESE QUESTIONS

Put an *x* in the box next to the correct answer.

Reading Comprehension

1. Skiff Miller's face got red because he was
- ❏ **a.** tired.
- ❏ **b.** sick.
- ❏ **c.** angry.

2. Which sentence is correct?
- ❏ **a.** Walt was stronger than Miller.
- ❏ **b.** Walt was shorter than Miller.
- ❏ **c.** Walt was taller than Miller.

3. Madge said Wolf barked because he was
- ❏ **a.** happy.
- ❏ **b.** sad.
- ❏ **c.** angry.

4. Madge asked Skiff Miller if he would
- ❏ **a.** give the dog to them.
- ❏ **b.** let them have the dog for a week.
- ❏ **c.** sell the dog to them.

5. Miller looked for the dog for
- ❏ **a.** three years.
- ❏ **b.** five years.
- ❏ **c.** ten years.

6. Brown was
- ❏ **a.** very lazy.
- ❏ **b.** a good worker.
- ❏ **c.** not smart.

Vocabulary

7. Walt said that any dog from Alaska would obey Miller. When you *obey*, you
- ❏ **a.** do what you are told.
- ❏ **b.** do not listen.
- ❏ **c.** run away quickly.

8. When the dog was stolen, Miller felt sick. When something is *stolen,* it is
- ❏ **a.** lost.
- ❏ **b.** found.
- ❏ **c.** taken away.

9. Miller raised his fist and took a step toward Walt. What part of the body is the *fist*?
- ❏ **a.** the head
- ❏ **b.** the hand
- ❏ **c.** the neck

Idioms

10. Wolf was friendly to Skiff Miller right away. The idiom *right away* means
- ❏ **a.** at once.
- ❏ **b.** much later.
- ❏ **c.** never.

How many questions did you answer correctly? Circle your score. Then fill in your score on the Score Chart on page 168.

Number Correct	1	2	3	4	5	6	7	8	9	10
Score	10	20	30	40	50	60	70	80	90	100

Exercises to Help You

Exercise A

Understanding the story. Answer each question by writing a complete sentence. Begin each sentence with a capital letter. End each sentence with a period. You may use the line numbers in parentheses to find the answers.

1. Why did Skiff Miller's face become red? (7)

2. When Miller took a step toward Walt, what did Madge do? (15)

3. Why did Wolf bark for the first time? (19)

4. What was Wolf's real name? (22)

5. How did Miller feel when Wolf was stolen? (30)

6. How long did Miller look for Wolf? (31)

7. What did the dog do while Miller and Madge were speaking? (48)

Exercise B

Building sentences. Make sentences by adding the correct letter.

1. _____ Walt thought that any dog from Alaska		**a.** best dog Miller ever had.
2. _____ Skiff Miller		**b.** sell the dog to them.
3. _____ Madge asked Miller if he would		**c.** stared down at Walt.
4. _____ Brown was the		**d.** would listen to Miller.

Now write the sentences on the lines below. Remember to begin each sentence with a capital letter and to end each sentence with a period.

1. _____

_____

2. _____

3. _____

_____

4. _____

Now do questions 5–8 the same way.

5. _____ When he saw the dog, Miller		**a.** very hard worker.
6. _____ Brown was a		**b.** whatever the dog wanted.
7. _____ The dog's ears were		**c.** thought that he was dreaming.
8. _____ Miller said he would do		**d.** standing straight up.

5. _____

_____

6. _____

7. _____

8. _____

_____

Exercise C

Adding vocabulary. On the left are 8 words from the story. Complete each sentence by adding the correct word.

choose

1. When he couldn't find Brown, Miller felt _____.

leader

2. Madge said, "Let the dog _____ where he wants to live."

understands

3. Brown was the _____ of a team of dogs.

sick

4. The dog is so smart that he _____ you when you talk to him.

lazy

5. Wolf was probably _____ a lot of money.

worth

6. She said that Miller didn't _____ about the dog.

earned

7. The dog worked hard—he was never _____ .

care

8. Miller said, "The dog has _____ the right to choose."

Exercise D

Using verbs correctly. Fill in each blank using the **past tense** of the regular verb in parentheses. The first one has been done for you.

1. Walt said, "Maybe he ___*pulled*___ a sled for you once." (pull)

2. The dog _____ to Skiff Miller. (listen)

3. Miller _____ his fist and took a step toward Walt. (raise)

4. Madge _____ between the two men. (step)

5. She _____ to Miller and began to speak. (turn)

6. "Would you sell the dog to us?" she _____. (ask)

7. Brown _____ hard because he was not lazy. (work)

8. The dog _____ at Skiff Miller and Madge. (look)

Exercise E

Picking a pronoun. Fill in the blanks by adding the correct pronoun. Each sentence tells something about the story. Use each pronoun once.

I	we
you	you
he, she, it	they

1. Miller opened his mouth, but _____ didn't say anything.

2. Madge was afraid the men would fight, so _____ stepped between them.

3. Miller said, "When _____ saw the dog, I thought I was dreaming."

4. Walt told Miller, "You say the dog is yours, but _____ can't prove that."

5. Madge and Walt loved Wolf, so _____ tried to buy the dog from Skiff Miller.

6. Madge said, "If you will sell the dog to us, _____ would like to buy him."

7. Madge told Miller " _____ don't care about this dog."

8. Keep reading this story to see if _____ has a happy ending.

Exercise F

Vocabulary review. Write a complete sentence for each word or group of words.

1. obey _____

   _____

2. fist _____

   _____

3. stolen _____

   _____

4. worth _____

_____

5. leader _____

_____

6. choose _____

_____

7. lazy _____

_____

8. earned _____

_____

9. right away _____

_____

SHARING WITH OTHERS

It is fun to share ideas with others. Discuss these questions with your partner or with the group. Write your answer to one of the questions.

◆ If you could choose any place in the world to live, what place would you pick? Why?
◆ What countries have you lived in? Tell something about the country you know best.

_____

_____

_____

_____

_____

_____

PART 5

"Yes," Skiff Miller said again. "The dog has earned the right to choose. I'll do whatever he wants."

Madge smiled. "I think that's fair," she said.

Skiff Miller shook his head. Then he said, "Don't move. Stay where you are. I'll say good-bye. Then I'll walk away. If the dog wants to stay here, he can stay. But if he wants to go with me, let him go. I won't call him. I won't say a word. Don't call him either. Don't say a word to him. Let's see what he does."

"**All right**," said Madge. Walt nodded yes.

"I'm leaving now," Skiff Miller said loudly. "Good-bye." He walked up to Madge and Walt. He **shook hands** with them. Then he began to walk away.

The dog was lying on his side. He watched the three people. He saw them shake hands. He heard Skiff Miller say good-bye.

Wolf lifted his head. He stood up. He watched Miller walk away. He waited for Miller to come back. But Miller kept walking.

Wolf ran down the road. He stopped in front of Miller. He tried to stand in Miller's way. Miller said nothing. He walked around the dog.

Wolf ran back to Walt. The dog **grabbed** Walt's pant leg with his teeth. He tried to **drag** Walt toward Skiff Miller. But Walt did not move.

Wolf let go of Walt's leg. He ran down the road toward Miller. Then he ran back to Walt and Madge. He ran up to Madge. She did not speak. She did not touch him.

The dog backed away. He turned around and looked at Miller. The man was still walking. He was moving further away.

Wolf ran down the road. Suddenly he stopped. He raised his head. He barked. He barked again. But Skiff Miller kept walking.

Wolf ran back to Walt and Madge. He barked at them. They did not move.

Wolf looked back at Miller. He watched the man. The man was at the curve at the end of the road. Wolf kept watching. Then Miller was gone. Wolf could not see him.

Wolf lay down on his side. He did not move. He was waiting for Skiff Miller to come back. Wolf lay on his side and waited. He waited and waited.

"He's staying," said Madge. "He's staying!"

Suddenly Wolf got up. He did not look at the woman and the man. He was looking at the road. Wolf had **made up his mind**. He had chosen.

Wolf began to run. He ran down the road. He ran faster and faster. He did not look back. He ran straight ahead. A minute later, Wolf was gone.

YOU CAN ANSWER THESE QUESTIONS

Put an *x* in the box next to the correct answer.

Reading Comprehension

1. Skiff Miller said that he would
   - ❏ **a.** make the dog go with him.
   - ❏ **b.** give the dog to Walt and Madge.
   - ❏ **c.** let the dog choose.

2. Miller told Madge and Walt
   - ❏ **a.** to call the dog.
   - ❏ **b.** not to call the dog.
   - ❏ **c.** to send a letter to him in Alaska.

3. When Wolf ran up to Madge, she
   - ❏ **a.** spoke to him.
   - ❏ **b.** touched him.
   - ❏ **c.** did not speak to him or touch him.

4. What was Wolf waiting for?
   - ❏ **a.** He was waiting for Miller to come back.
   - ❏ **b.** He was waiting for Madge to feed him.
   - ❏ **c.** He was waiting for Walt to bring him some water.

5. At the end of the story, Wolf
   - ❏ **a.** stayed with Madge and Walt.
   - ❏ **b.** ran after Skiff Miller.
   - ❏ **c.** began to cry.

Vocabulary

6. The dog grabbed Walt's pant leg. When you *grab* some thing, you
   - ❏ **a.** fix it.
   - ❏ **b.** hold on to it tightly.
   - ❏ **c.** let it go.

7. Wolf tried to drag Walt toward Miller. The word *drag* means
   - ❏ **a.** pull.
   - ❏ **b.** throw.
   - ❏ **c.** hurt.

Idioms

8. When Miller told them what to do, Madge said, "All right." When you say *all right*, you mean
   - ❏ **a.** yes.
   - ❏ **b.** no.
   - ❏ **c.** maybe.

9. Miller shook hands with Walt and Madge and walked away. People *shake hands* when they
   - ❏ **a.** talk on the telephone.
   - ❏ **b.** say hello or good-bye.
   - ❏ **c.** watch television.

10. At the end of the story, Wolf made up his mind. When you *make up your mind*, you
    - ❏ **a.** don't know what to do.
    - ❏ **b.** choose or decide.
    - ❏ **c.** feel sad.

How many questions did you answer correctly? Circle your score. Then fill in your score on the Score Chart on page 168.

Number Correct	1	2	3	4	5	6	7	8	9	10
Score	10	20	30	40	50	60	70	80	90	100

Exercises to Help You

Exercise A

Understanding the story. Answer each question by writing a complete sentence. Begin each sentence with a capital letter. End each sentence with a period. You may use the line numbers in parentheses to find the answers.

1. What did Skiff Miller do after he shook hands with Madge and Walt? (12)

   _____

2. What did the dog hear Skiff Miller say? (14)

   _____

3. When Wolf stood in front of Miller, what did Miller do? (18)

   _____

4. What happened when the dog tried to drag Walt toward Miller? (20)

   _____

5. What happened when the dog ran up to Madge? (24)

   _____

6. Who was Wolf waiting for? (35)

   _____

7. What did Wolf do at the end of the story? (41)

   _____

Exercise B

Building sentences. Make sentences by adding the correct letter.

1. _____ The dog was   **a.** shake hands.
2. _____ Wolf saw the three people   **b.** the end of the road.
3. _____ Miller walked   **c.** lying on his side.
4. _____ The man was at   **d.** around the dog.

Now write the sentences on the lines below. Remember to begin each sentence with a capital letter and to end each sentence with a period.

1. _____

2. _____

   _____

3. _____

4. _____

   _____

Now do questions 5–8 the same way.

5. _____ Wolf could not   **a.** the woman and the man.

6. _____ Madge thought that Wolf   **b.** faster and faster down the road.

7. _____ The dog did not look at   **c.** was staying.
8. _____ He ran   **d.** see the man.

5. _____

6. _____

7. _____

   _____

8. _____

   _____

Exercise C

Adding vocabulary. On the left are 6 words from the story. Complete each sentence by adding the correct word.

straight

1. The dog ran _____ ahead.

curve

2. Wolf _____ stopped running and raised his head.

minute

3. Skiff Miller came to the _____ at the end of the road.

suddenly

teeth

4. The dog held on to the pant leg with his _____ .

nodded

5. Walt _____ yes.

6. A _____ later, Wolf was gone.

Exercise D

Using verbs correctly. Fill in each blank using the **past tense** of the irregular verb in parentheses. The first one has been done for you.

1. The dog _____*ran*_____ down the road. (run)

2. Wolf _____ the man say good-bye. (hear)

3. He _____ Skiff Miller leave. (see)

4. Suddenly the dog _____ up. (get)

5. "I think that's fair," Madge _____. (say)

6. Wolf lifted his head and _____ up. (stand)

Exercise E

Putting words in correct order. Make sentences by putting the words in the correct order. Write each sentence on the line. The first one has been done for you.

1. lifted / head / his / Wolf

    Wolf lifted his head.   .

2. ran / the / road / Wolf / down

    _____ .

3. not / Walt / move /did

    _____ .

4. hands / shook / Miller / them / with

    _____ .

5. him / Madge / to / not / speak / did

    _____ .

Exercise F

Vocabulary review. Write a complete sentence for each word or group of words.

1. grabbed _____

   _____

2. drag _____

   _____

3. curve _____

_____

4. nodded _____

_____

5. all right _____

_____

6. shake hands _____

_____

7. make up (her or his) mind _____

_____

SHARING WITH OTHERS

It is fun to share ideas with others. Discuss these questions with your partner or with the group. Write your answer to one of the questions.

◆ Were you glad that the dog went with Skiff Miller—or did you want the dog to stay with Madge and Walt? Why?
◆ Why do you think the dog went with Miller?

_____

_____

_____

_____

_____

_____

CRUCITA

by Manuela Williams Crosno

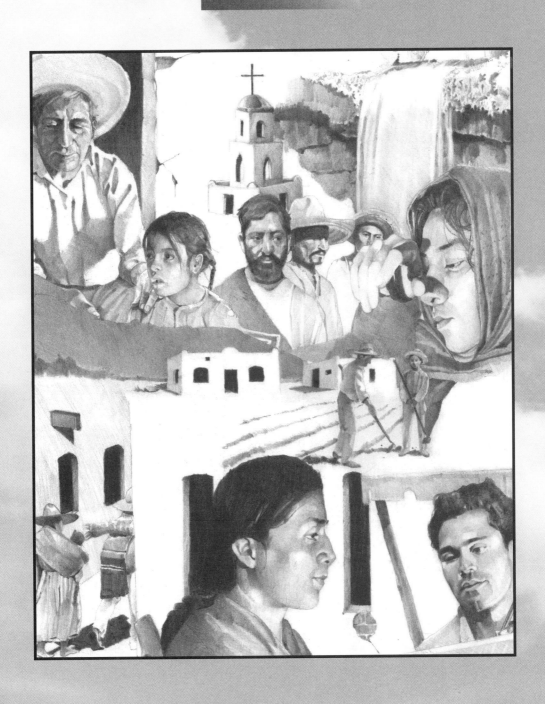

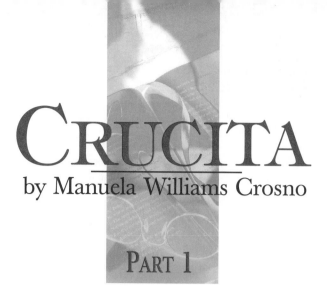

CRUCITA

by Manuela Williams Crosno

PART 1

Crucita Valdéz lived in a small village called San Eliso. The village was near a river named the Rio Grande.

Crucita had two sisters. They were named Isabella and Rosita. They were very beautiful.

5 Crucita, however, was not beautiful. She had large black eyes. But they were always half-closed. She also walked in a very strange way.

One day Crucita was sitting on the steps of her house. She was five years old. Crucita's grandfather, Filiberto, looked at her. He said
10 softly to himself, "Ah, Crucita. It is too bad you do not look like your sisters."

Crucita could hear very well. She said, "What do I look like, Grandpa?"

Filiberto was surprised. He did not think Crucita could hear his
15 words.

He told Crucita, "You are kind to me. You are kind to everyone. You help your parents. You always do good things. You are a wonderful child, Crucita."

There was a church in the middle of the village. The church was
20 the biggest building in the village. People prayed in the church. It was the meeting place for the villagers. **Every so often** there were parties in the church. The church was very important to the people of San Eliso.

The church was very old. When it rained, the roof **leaked**. Cold winds blew through the walls. The people of San Eliso wanted a new church. But the villagers were poor. They did not have much money. They could not **afford** to build a new church.

One day Sister Mary Olivia was in the church. Crucita was with her. They were looking at a book. Sister Mary Olivia was showing Crucita some words in the book.

Crucita said, "Sister Mary, I cannot see the words. The words are very small. They are too small for me to see."

Then Sister Mary **realized** that Crucita could hardly see. She was almost blind. That is why her eyes were always half-closed. That is why she walked in a strange way.

Put an *x* in the box next to the correct answer.

Reading Comprehension

1. Crucita Valdéz lived in a
- ❏ **a.** big city.
- ❏ **b.** large town.
- ❏ **c.** small village.

2. Crucita's sisters were very
- ❏ **a.** old.
- ❏ **b.** young.
- ❏ **c.** beautiful.

3. Crucita's eyes were always
- ❏ **a.** wide open.
- ❏ **b.** half-closed.
- ❏ **c.** very red.

4. Filiberto said that Crucita
- ❏ **a.** was kind and helpful.
- ❏ **b.** loved to play games.
- ❏ **c.** always got into trouble.

5. The church was the
- ❏ **a.** smallest building in the village.
- ❏ **b.** biggest building in the village.
- ❏ **c.** newest building in the village.

6. Crucita walked in a strange way because
- ❏ **a.** her legs hurt her.
- ❏ **b.** she was five years old.
- ❏ **c.** she had trouble seeing.

Vocabulary

7. The church was old. When it rained, the roof leaked. When a roof *leaks,* it
- ❏ **a.** keeps the building warm.
- ❏ **b.** lets the rain in.
- ❏ **c.** keeps the rain out.

8. The people of the village were poor. They could not afford to build a new church. The word *afford* means to have enough
- ❏ **a.** time for.
- ❏ **b.** money for.
- ❏ **c.** room for.

9. Crucita said that the words were very small. Then Sister Mary realized that Crucita could hardly see. The word *realized* means
- ❏ **a.** found out.
- ❏ **b.** forgot.
- ❏ **c.** asked about.

Idioms

10. Every so often there were parties in the church. The idiom *every so often* means
- ❏ **a.** sometimes.
- ❏ **b.** once a year.
- ❏ **c.** every morning and night.

How many questions did you answer correctly? Circle your score. Then fill in your score on the Score Chart on page 168.

Number Correct	1	2	3	4	5	6	7	8	9	10
Score	10	20	30	40	50	60	70	80	90	100

Exercise A

Understanding the story. Answer each question by writing a complete sentence. Begin each sentence with a capital letter. End each sentence with a period. You may use the line numbers in parentheses to find the answers.

1. Where did Crucita Valdéz live? (1)

   _____

2. How many sisters did Crucita have? (3)

   _____

3. Was Crucita beautiful? (5)

   _____

4. How did Crucita walk? (6)

   _____

5. Why was Filiberto surprised? (14)

   _____

   _____

6. How big was the church? (20)

   _____

   _____

7. What did the people of San Eliso want? (25)

   _____

   _____

8. What did Sister Mary find out? (33)

   _____

   _____

Exercise B

Building sentences. Make sentences by adding the correct letter.

1. _____ Crucita Valdéz had		**a.**	could hear his words.
2. _____ One day Crucita was sitting		**b.**	a wonderful child.
3. _____ Filiberto did not think that Crucita		**c.**	on the steps of her house.
4. _____ He said that she was		**d.**	large black eyes.

Now write the sentences on the lines below. Remember to begin each sentence with a capital letter and to end each sentence with a period.

1. _____

2. _____

_____

3. _____

_____

4. _____

Now do questions 5–8 the same way.

5. _____ The church was the		**a.**	some words in a book.
6. _____ It was very important to		**b.**	meeting place for the villagers.
7. _____ Cold winds blew		**c.**	the people of San Eliso.
8. _____ Sister Mary was showing Crucita		**d.**	through the walls.

5. _____

_____

6. _____

_____

7. _____

8. _____

_____

Exercise C

Adding vocabulary. On the left are 6 words from the story. Complete each sentence by adding the correct word.

child

blind

parents

church

middle

prayed

1. One day Sister Mary Olivia was in the _____ .

2. Filiberto thought that Crucita was

   a wonderful _____.

3. The church was in the _____ of the village.

4. People _____ in the church.

5. Crucita always helped her _____.

6. She could hardly see; she was almost _____.

Exercise D

Part A

True or false sentences. Write **T** if the sentence is true. Write **F** if the sentence is false. On the lines below, correct the false sentences.

1. _____ The village was near a river named the Rio Grande.

2. _____ The village was called Santa Fe.

3. _____ Crucita could not hear very well.

4. _____ The people of the village did not want a new church.

5. _____ Crucita said she could not see the words.

Part B

On the lines below, correct the false sentences.

a. _____

b. _____

c. _____

_____

Exercise E

Part A

Adding an adjective. Complete the sentences below by writing the correct adjective. Each sentence tells something about the story. Use each adjective once.

new   small   wonderful   beautiful   strange

1. Crucita Valdéz lived in a _____ village.

2. The church was old, but the people could not build a _____ church.

3. Since she could not see well, Crucita walked in a _____ way.

4. Filiberto told Crucita, "You are a _____ child."

5. Crucita's sisters were _____ .

Part B

Here are some other adjectives from the story. On the lines below, write your own sentences using these adjectives.

kind   large   old   good   cold

1. _____

2. _____

3. _____

4. _____

5. _____

Exercise F

Vocabulary review. Write a complete sentence for each word or group of words.

1. parents _____

_____

2. blind _____

_____

3. prayed _____

_____

4. leaked _____

_____

5. afford _____

_____

6. realized _____

_____

7. every so often _____

_____

SHARING WITH OTHERS

It is fun to share ideas with others. Discuss these questions with your partner or with the group. Write your answer to one of the questions.

◆ Why do you think Crucita could hear so well?
◆ Crucita asked, "What do I look like, Grandpa?" Her grandfather answered, "You are a wonderful child." Do you think the five-year-old child was happy with the answer? Why?

_____

_____

_____

_____

_____

PART 2

Crucita could not see well. Still, she was happy. She loved to play in the forest. The animals were her friends. Birds ate from her hand. Rabbits and squirrels ran to her when she called.

One morning Crucita woke up very early. At breakfast she
5   looked worried. She said, "Papa, last night I had a strange dream. I dreamed that Ricardo and Hermano were on a mountain. They were **trapped** on the mountain. They could not get down. They were in trouble."

Ricardo and Hermano were brothers. They were very wild. They
10   often went into the mountains.

Señor Valdéz said, "Do not worry, Crucita. I am sure that Ricardo and Hermano are all right. I am sure they are safe. You had a bad dream. It was only a dream."

That afternoon some men rode up to the house. They got off
15   their horses. They ran up to the house. They were **in a hurry**.

Señor Valdéz met the men. "What is wrong?" he asked.

One man said, "We are looking for Ricardo and Hermano. They are lost. We have looked for them for two days. We have not found them **so far**."

20   Another man said, "We thought they were fishing in a boat. We rode along the side of the river. But we did not see them. Have you seen Ricardo and Hermano?"

Señor Valdéz said, "Perhaps I can help you." He told the men about Crucita's dream. Then he called his daughter. He asked her,
25   "Do you remember your dream? Where were Ricardo and Hermano? Where were they trapped? Where was the place?"

Crucita thought for a moment. Then she said, "They were on a little path that was very narrow. The path was like a ledge. It was near the top of a mountain. It was behind a tall waterfall."

30 One man said, "I know that place. Let's go!"

The men got on their horses. They rode toward the mountain.

The men got to the mountain just before dark. They looked up at the waterfall. They called up to the brothers.

A moment later they heard shouts. "Help! Help!" yelled the boys.

35 The men climbed up the mountain. They brought down the two brothers. Later the boys told what happened. They were climbing near the top of the mountain. Suddenly their rope broke. They fell and landed on the narrow path. Ricardo had **twisted** his ankle. Hermano had hurt his knee. They could not walk.

40 But now both boys were safe.

The brothers and their family thanked Señor Valdéz. "Do not thank me," said Señor Valdéz. "Thank Crucita. She is the one who saved the boys."

YOU CAN ANSWER THESE QUESTIONS

Put an *x* in the box next to the correct answer.

Reading Comprehension

1. Crucita loved to
   - ❑ **a.** read many books.
   - ❑ **b.** play in the forest.
   - ❑ **c.** go to the store.

2. Crucita looked worried because she
   - ❑ **a.** was feeling sick.
   - ❑ **b.** had a fight with her sisters.
   - ❑ **c.** had a strange dream.

3. The men looked for Ricardo and Hermano for
   - ❑ **a.** two days.
   - ❑ **b.** two weeks.
   - ❑ **c.** two months.

4. Crucita dreamed that Ricardo and Hermano were
   - ❑ **a.** fishing from a boat.
   - ❑ **b.** walking in a valley.
   - ❑ **c.** on a little path near the top of a mountain.

5. The boys were not able to
   - ❑ **a.** walk.
   - ❑ **b.** talk.
   - ❑ **c.** move their arms.

6. Señor Valdéz said that
   - ❑ **a.** he saved the boys.
   - ❑ **b.** Crucita saved the boys.
   - ❑ **c.** the men saved the boys.

Vocabulary

7. The boys were trapped on the mountain. When you are *trapped*, you are
   - ❑ **a.** safe.
   - ❑ **b.** with friends.
   - ❑ **c.** not able to get away.

8. Ricardo fell and twisted his ankle. The word *twisted* means
   - ❑ **a.** turned.
   - ❑ **b.** fixed.
   - ❑ **c.** watched.

Idioms

9. The men ran up to the house because they were in a hurry. When you are *in a hurry,* you
   - ❑ **a.** move slowly.
   - ❑ **b.** move quickly.
   - ❑ **c.** feel happy.

10. A man said, "We have not found the boys so far." The idiom *so far* means
    - ❑ **a.** in the air.
    - ❑ **b.** on any side.
    - ❑ **c.** up to now.

How many questions did you answer correctly? Circle your score. Then fill in your score on the Score Chart on page 168.

Number Correct	1	2	3	4	5	6	7	8	9	10
Score	10	20	30	40	50	60	70	80	90	100

EXERCISES TO HELP YOU

Exercise A

Understanding the story. Answer each question by writing a complete sentence. Begin each sentence with a capital letter. End each sentence with a period. You may use the line numbers in parentheses to find the answers.

1. What did Crucita love to do? (1)

   _____

2. Who were Crucita's friends? (2)

   _____

3. Why did Crucita look worried? (5)

   _____

   _____

4. What did Crucita dream? (6)

   _____

   _____

5. Who were the men looking for? (17)

   _____

   _____

6. Where did the men ride? (31)

   _____

7. What happened to the rope? (37)

   _____

8. Who saved the boys? (42)

   _____

Exercise B

Building sentences. Make sentences by adding the correct letter.

1. _____ Crucita could not		**a.**	the boys were safe.
2. _____ Ricardo and Hermano were		**b.**	see well.
3. _____ Señor Valdéz believed that		**c.**	the side of the river.
4. _____ The men rode along		**d.**	very wild.

Now write the sentences on the lines below. Remember to begin each sentence with a capital letter and to end each sentence with a period.

1. _____

2. _____

3. _____

_____

4. _____

_____

Now do questions 5–8 the same way.

5. _____ Señor Valdéz told the men		**a.**	just before dark.
6. _____ She said the boys were near		**b.**	on the path.
7. _____ The men got to the mountain		**c.**	about Crucita's dream.
8. _____ The boys fell and landed		**d.**	the top of a mountain.

5. _____

_____

6. _____

_____

7. _____

_____

8. _____

Exercise C

Adding vocabulary. On the left are 5 words and an idiom from the story. Complete each sentence by adding the correct word or words.

climbed

remember

squirrels

narrow

all right

ledge

1. Rabbits and _____ ran to Crucita when she called.

2. Señor Valdéz thought that Ricardo and Hermano were _____ .

3. He asked Crucita, "Do you _____ your dream?"

4. The men _____ up the mountain and found the boys.

5. The boys were on a little path that was like a _____.

6. The path was not wide; it was _____.

Exercise D

Using verbs correctly. Fill in each blank using the **past tense** of the irregular verb in parentheses.

1. Birds _____ from Crucita's hand. (eat)

2. One morning Crucita _____ up very early. (wake)

3. That afternoon some men _____ up to the house. (ride)

4. Señor Valdéz _____ the men. (meet)

5. They _____ not see Ricardo or Hermano. (do)

6. The men _____ the brothers down from the mountain. (bring)

7. The boys said that their rope _____. (break)

Exercise E

Changing statements to questions. Change each statement to a question that begins with *Who*. Put a question mark at the end of each question. The first one has been done for you.

1. Crucita could not see well.

   Who could not see well?

2. Rabbits and squirrels ran to Crucita when she called.

   _____

3. Ricardo and Hermano were brothers.

   _____

4. Señor Valdéz told Crucita not to worry.

   _____

5. That afternoon some men rode up to the house.

   _____

6. The boys told them what happened.

   _____

7. The brothers and their family thanked Señor Valdéz.

   _____

Exercise F

Vocabulary review. Write a complete sentence for each word or group of words.

1. squirrels _____

   _____

2. narrow _____

   _____

3. climbed _____

_____

4. ledge _____

_____

5. trapped _____

_____

6. twisted _____

_____

7. all right _____

_____

8. in a hurry _____

_____

9. so far _____

_____

SHARING WITH OTHERS

It is fun to share ideas with others. Discuss these questions with your partner or with the group. Write your answer to one of the questions.

◆ A terrible dream is called a nightmare. Why does a nightmare always wake you up?

◆ Do you think Ricardo and Hermano will go back into the mountains soon? Why?

_____

_____

_____

_____

_____

PART 3

It was a day in spring. Crucita was eating dinner with her parents. Suddenly Crucita said, "I think we should plant the crops[1] soon. I think we should plant them next week."

Crucita's father was surprised. "Next week?" he said. "That is
5   very early."

"Yes," said Crucita.

Crucita's mother asked, "Why should we plant so early this year?"

"I do not know," said Crucita. "But I think it is a good idea."
10   Señor Valdéz thought for a moment. He turned to his wife. "We never plant so early," he said. "But let us listen to Crucita."

The next week Señor Valdéz began to plant his crops. A neighbor saw him and said, "Why are you planting so early?"

Señor Valdéz told him what Crucita had said.
15   "You must be joking," said the neighbor. "You are planting now because of Crucita?"

"Yes," said Señor Valdéz.

"I see," said the neighbor. At first he thought Señor Valdéz was wrong to plant so early. But then he thought about Crucita. He had
20   heard about her dream. He remembered how she saved Ricardo and Hermano.

The next day he began to plant his crops.

Before long all the farmers in the village were planting their crops.
25   Everything grew very well that year. Everything came up early. One by one the farmers **gathered** their crops. Finally all the crops were in.

Señor Valdéz was sitting in the living room with his wife. He was happy. He told his wife, "The crop was very good this year."

1. *crops:* plants that are grown for food.

Just then Crucita's sisters ran into the house.

"Look outside!" said Isabella.

"Yes, look outside!" shouted Rosita.

Everyone ran to the window. They looked outside.

They saw a huge black cloud. The cloud was moving toward the village. **All at once** it got very dark. There was a loud crash. Then it began to rain. It rained very hard. It rained harder and harder. The rain mixed with ice. The **hail** crashed down everywhere.

The hail made loud noises on the roof. It broke some windows in the house. It crashed down on the empty fields.

Then, suddenly, the terrible storm was over. The sun came out. The day began to get brighter.

Señor Valdéz said, "I am glad we planted early. The storm would have **destroyed** the crops."

Crucita was standing at the window.

"Look," she said. "A rainbow."

Everyone looked outside. They saw a beautiful rainbow in the sky.

YOU CAN ANSWER THESE QUESTIONS

Put an *x* in the box next to the correct answer.

Reading Comprehension

1. Crucita thought they should plant the crops
   - ❏ **a.** in a month.
   - ❏ **b.** in two weeks.
   - ❏ **c.** next week.

2. When Crucita said they should plant early, her father was
   - ❏ **a.** angry.
   - ❏ **b.** surprised.
   - ❏ **c.** happy.

3. Which sentence is true?
   - ❏ **a.** None of the other farmers planted early.
   - ❏ **b.** Some of the other farmers planted early.
   - ❏ **c.** All of the other farmers planted early.

4. Señor Valdéz told his wife that the crop was
   - ❏ **a.** very good that year.
   - ❏ **b.** very bad that year.
   - ❏ **c.** the same as last year's crop.

5. A huge black cloud
   - ❏ **a.** moved toward the village.
   - ❏ **b.** moved away from the village.
   - ❏ **c.** broke some windows in the house.

6. After the storm was over, they saw
   - ❏ **a.** the moon.
   - ❏ **b.** many bright stars.
   - ❏ **c.** a beautiful rainbow.

Vocabulary

7. After everything came up, the farmers gathered their crops. The word *gathered* means
   - ❏ **a.** threw away.
   - ❏ **b.** brought in.
   - ❏ **c.** fell over.

8. During the storm, the hail made loud noises on the roof. What is *hail*?
   - ❏ **a.** snow
   - ❏ **b.** clouds
   - ❏ **c.** small pieces of ice

9. The storm would have destroyed the crops. The word *destroyed* means
   - ❏ **a.** helped.
   - ❏ **b.** warned.
   - ❏ **c.** killed.

Idioms

10. All at once, it got very dark. The idiom *all at once* means
    - ❏ **a.** suddenly.
    - ❏ **b.** later.
    - ❏ **c.** at night.

How many questions did you answer correctly? Circle your score. Then fill in your score on the Score Chart on page 168.

Number Correct	1	2	3	4	5	6	7	8	9	10
Score	10	20	30	40	50	60	70	80	90	100

EXERCISES TO HELP YOU

Exercise A

Understanding the story. Answer each question by writing a complete sentence. Begin each sentence with a capital letter. End each sentence with a period. You may use the line numbers in parentheses to find the answers.

1. What did Crucita tell her parents at dinner? (2)

_____

2. When did Señor Valdéz begin to plant his crops? (12)

_____

_____

3. What did a neighbor ask Señor Valdéz? (13)

_____

_____

4. When did the neighbor begin to plant his crops? (22)

_____

_____

5. How did everything grow that year? (25)

_____

6. How hard did it rain? (36)

_____

7. What did the hail break? (38)

_____

_____

8. After the storm was over, what did they see in the sky? (46)

_____

Exercise B

Building sentences. Make sentences by adding the correct letter.

1. _____ Crucita was eating dinner
   a. they should plant so early that year.

2. _____ Her mother wanted to know why
   b. Crucita's dream.

3. _____ The neighbor had heard about
   c. saved Ricardo and Hermano.

4. _____ He remembered how Crucita
   d. with her parents.

Now write the sentences on the lines below. Remember to begin each sentence with a capital letter and to end each sentence with a period.

1. _____

2. _____

   _____

3. _____

4. _____

Now do questions 5–8 the same way.

5. _____ Señor Valdéz was sitting
   a. and looked outside.

6. _____ Everyone ran to the window
   b. the sun came out.

7. _____ The pieces of hail
   c. in the living room with his wife.

8. _____ When the storm was over,
   d. crashed down everywhere.

5. _____

   _____

6. _____

   _____

7. _____

8. _____

Exercise C

Adding vocabulary. On the left are 5 words and an idiom from the story. Complete each sentence by adding the correct word or words.

listen

at first

joking

idea

huge

crash

1. Crucita thought it was a good _____ to plant early.

2. Señor Valdéz told his wife, "Let us _____ to Crucita."

3. A neighbor said, "You must be _____ to plant now because of Crucita."

4. They looked outside and saw a _____ black cloud.

5. There was a loud _____ and then it began to rain.

6. The neighbor thought, _____, that Señor Valdéz was wrong to plant so early.

Exercise D

Using verbs correctly. Fill in each blank using the **past tense** of the irregular verb in parentheses.

1. Señor Valdéz _____ the neighbor what Crucita had said. (tell)

2. The neighbor _____ that Señor Valdéz was wrong to plant so early. (think)

3. The farmers were happy because everything _____ well that year. (grow)

4. After the storm was over, the sun _____ out. (come)

5. The day _____ to get brighter. (begin)

Exercise E

Putting words in correct order. Make sentences by putting the words in the correct order. Write each sentence on the line.

1. spring / was / It / a / day / in

   _____.

2. crops / The / up / early / came

   _____.

3. house / ran / sisters / Crucita's / the / into

   _____.

4. rainbow / saw / beautiful / a / They

   _____.

5. over / storm / terrible / was / The / suddenly

   _____.

Exercise F

Vocabulary review. Write a complete sentence for each word or group of words.

1. crash _____

   _____

2. huge _____

   _____

3. joking _____

   _____

4. gathered _____

   _____

5. hail _____

_____

6. destroyed _____

_____

7. at first _____

_____

8. all at once _____

_____

SHARING WITH OTHERS

It is fun to share ideas with others. Discuss these questions with your partner or with the group. Write your answer to one of the questions.

◆ Why do you think all the farmers planted early? Later, were they glad they did? Why?

◆ At the end of Part Three, the family saw a beautiful rainbow in the sky. What does this mean? What do you think the writer is saying?

_____

_____

_____

_____

_____

_____

_____

PART 4

One day Sister Mary Olivia **called on** Crucita at her house. Sister Mary asked Crucita if she would help at the church. Crucita said, "Yes. I would like to help."

Crucita kept the church clean. She always kept a candle burning. She planted a garden next to the church. She grew corn, beans, and grapes in the garden. She also planted many beautiful flowers.

Over the years many people visited the garden. It was a quiet, peaceful place. Crucita had a warm smile for everyone. She helped the old and the ill. She played with the children who came to visit her. Everyone knew and loved Crucita.

One morning Crucita went to see Sister Mary. Crucita said, "Sister, I know you sometimes go to Santa Fe. Are you going there soon?"

Sister Mary said, "Yes. I must buy some things in Santa Fe. Why do you want to know?"

Crucita said, "I would like to go to Santa Fe with you."

Sister Mary said, "Let us go today. I will speak to Father Isidro. We can leave at once."

An hour later they were ready to leave. Father Isidro came by with a wagon and a team of mules. He also brought a driver. The four people began their long **journey**.

After several hours they got to Santa Fe. The wagon stopped at the Plaza in town.

Crucita said, "I would like to walk around the Plaza."

Sister Mary Olivia said, "We will meet you here later." Then she and Father Isidro went into some stores.

Crucita had heard about the Plaza. She knew that it had many interesting shops. Crucita could not see well, so she walked very, very slowly. Still, she **bumped** into a man.

The man was sitting on a chair. He was drawing a picture of the Plaza.

"Excuse me," said Crucita.

"No, no," said the man. "It is my fault. My chair was in the way."

The man got up from his chair. Then he bowed to Crucita.

35 The man said, "I am an **artist**. I came here from Mexico City. I am drawing pictures of the Plaza. I also draw some of the people I see."

The man looked at Crucita. "May I draw you?" he asked.

"If you wish," said Crucita.

40 "Please sit here," said the man. He pointed to the chair. Crucita sat down. The man began to draw.

The man worked for a long time. Crucita sat very still. The man and Crucita spoke to each other. Crucita told him about the village of San Eliso. She told him about the old church. She told him about

45 her garden.

Finally he was finished. An hour had passed.

Just then Crucita heard a voice. It was Sister Mary Olivia. "We are ready to go home," she said.

Crucita said good-bye to the artist. Then she joined Father Isidro

50 and Sister Mary. They got into the wagon. Then they left for San Eliso.

Five years went by. Crucita continued to help the old and the poor. She was a friend to the young. People called her "Crucita the Good."

55 Then one day a letter arrived at the village. The letter came from Mexico City. A famous artist there had sent the letter. He was the man who had drawn Crucita in the Plaza. The letter said:

I know about your village. I am sending you money. Tear down the old church. Build a new church there. Do not touch the garden.

60 *I am sending you a stained glass window.[1] Please use it in the church.*

The new church was finished six months later. One window was made of stained glass. This window was made by the artist from Mexico City. It showed the face of a young woman. Sunlight came

65 through the window. The face shone brightly.

People looked at the face and said, "How beautiful she is. She looks just like Crucita!"

---

1. *stained glass window:* a window made in many colors.

YOU CAN ANSWER THESE QUESTIONS

Put an *x* in the box next to the correct answer.

Reading Comprehension

1. Sister Mary Olivia asked Crucita if she would
   - ❏ **a.** go to a meeting at the church.
   - ❏ **b.** give some money to the church.
   - ❏ **c.** help at the church.

2. What did Crucita grow in the garden?
   - ❏ **a.** apples
   - ❏ **b.** oranges
   - ❏ **c.** corn, beans, and grapes

3. Crucita said she wanted to
   - ❏ **a.** walk around the Plaza.
   - ❏ **b.** meet a friend in the Plaza.
   - ❏ **c.** buy something in the Plaza.

4. The man asked if he could
   - ❏ **a.** visit Crucita.
   - ❏ **b.** draw Crucita.
   - ❏ **c.** send a letter to Crucita.

5. The artist sent money to
   - ❏ **a.** fix up the garden.
   - ❏ **b.** build a new church.
   - ❏ **c.** buy books for the church.

6. The new church was finished
   - ❏ **a.** two months later.
   - ❏ **b.** four months later.
   - ❏ **c.** six months later.

Vocabulary

7. The man said, "I am an artist. I am drawing pictures of the Plaza." An *artist* is someone who
   - ❏ **a.** buys pictures.
   - ❏ **b.** paints pictures.
   - ❏ **c.** borrows pictures.

8. Crucita could not see well, so she bumped into a man who was sitting in a chair. When she *bumped* into the man, she
   - ❏ **a.** knocked against him.
   - ❏ **b.** asked about him.
   - ❏ **c.** cared about him.

9. The four people began their journey to Sante Fe. The word *journey* means
   - ❏ **a.** trip.
   - ❏ **b.** work.
   - ❏ **c.** train.

Idioms

10. Sister Mary called on Crucita at her house. The idiom *called on* means
    - ❏ **a.** yelled at.
    - ❏ **b.** shouted to.
    - ❏ **c.** visited.

How many questions did you answer correctly? Circle your score. Then fill in your score on the Score Chart on page 168.

Number Correct	1	2	3	4	5	6	7	8	9	10
Score	10	20	30	40	50	60	70	80	90	100

EXERCISES TO HELP YOU

Exercise A

Understanding the story. Answer each question by writing a complete sentence. Begin each sentence with a capital letter. End each sentence with a period. You may use the line numbers in parentheses to find the answers.

1. What did Sister Mary ask Crucita? (2)

   _____

   _____

2. What did Crucita say to Sister Mary? (3)

   _____

3. What did Crucita plant in the garden? (5)

   _____

   _____

4. What was the artist drawing? (36)

   _____

5. How long did the man work? (42)

   _____

6. What did Crucita tell the artist? (43)

   _____

   _____

7. What did the letter ask the villagers to build? (59)

   _____

8. What was one window made of? (63)

   _____

Exercise B

Building sentences. Make sentences by adding the correct letter.

1. _____ Crucita said that she was glad   **a.** visited the garden.
2. _____ She kept the   **b.** warm smile for everyone.
3. _____ Over the years many people   **c.** church clean.
4. _____ Crucita had a   **d.** to help.

Write the sentences on the lines below. Remember to begin each sentence with a capital letter and to end each sentence with a period.

1. _____

2. _____

3. _____

4. _____

Now do questions 5–8 the same way.

5. _____ Crucita played with the children   **a.** the artist from Mexico City.
6. _____ Sister Mary and Father Isidro went   **b.** was very beautiful.
7. _____ One window was made by   **c.** who came to visit her.
8. _____ The people thought that the face   **d.** into some shops.

5. _____

_____

6. _____

_____

7. _____

_____

8. _____

_____

Exercise C

Adding vocabulary. On the left are 7 words and an idiom from the story. Complete each sentence by adding the correct word or words.

wagon

joined

at once

mules

candle

famous

arrived

several

1. Crucita always kept a _____ burning in the church.

2. Sister Mary said, "Let us go today. We can leave_____."

3. An hour later Father Isidro came by with a _____.

4. He also brought a team of _____.

5. They got to Santa Fe after _____ hours.

6. Crucita said good-bye and then she _____ Sister Mary and Father Isidro.

7. One day a letter _____ at the village.

8. A _____ artist sent money to the people of San Eliso.

Exercise D

Picking a pronoun. Fill in the blanks by adding the correct pronoun. Each sentence tells something about the story. Use each pronoun once.

I	we
you	you
he, she, it	they

1. The man said, "_____ am an artist."

2. He got up from his chair. Then _____ bowed to Crucita.

3. He told Crucita, "_____ would be interesting to draw."

4. Crucita told him about the church. Then _____ told him about her garden.

5. Many people visited the garden because _____ was a quiet, peaceful place.

6. All of them got into the wagon. Then _____ left for San Eliso.

7. Sister Mary said, "Father Isidro will be here soon. Then _____ can all go to Santa Fe."

8. In his letter to the people, the man said, "I know _____ need money for a new church.

Exercise E

Changing statements to questions. Change each statement to a question that begins with *Where*. Put a question mark at the end of each question. The first one has been done for you.

1. Crucita planted the garden next to the church.

   Where did Crucita plant the garden?

2. Crucita wanted to go to Santa Fe.

   _____

3. The wagon stopped at the Plaza.

   _____

4. Crucita wanted to walk around the Plaza.

   _____

5. The artist came from Mexico City.

   _____

Exercise F

Vocabulary review. Write a complete sentence for each word or group of words.

1. wagon _____

   _____

2. joined _____

   _____

3. mules _____

_____

4. candle _____

_____

5. famous _____

_____

6. arrived _____

_____

7. several _____

_____

8. bumped _____

_____

9. artist _____

_____

10. journey _____

_____

11. called on _____

_____

SHARING WITH OTHERS

It is fun to share ideas with others. Discuss these questions with your partner or with the group. Write your answer to one of the questions.

◆ Why do you think the artist sent the stained glass window?
◆ Why did people think that Crucita was beautiful?

_____

_____

_____

The Last Leaf

by O. Henry

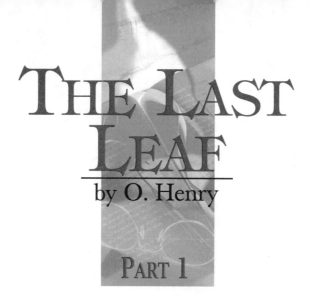

THE LAST LEAF

by O. Henry

PART 1

Sue and Joanna were friends. They lived together in a small apartment. It was in Greenwich Village in New York City.

Sue and Joanna were artists. They loved to paint.

Many artists live in Greenwich Village. Most of them are poor.
5   Sue and Joanna were poor, too. They saved their money to pay the rent. Although their apartment was small, they liked it very much. It had beautiful, big windows.

One day in November Joanna got sick. She felt very **weak**. She began to cough. She got into bed.
10   Day after day Joanna stayed in bed. She did not move. She did not eat. It was hard for her to breathe. Joanna stared out the window all day. **As soon as** she got up, she looked across the **alley** to the house next door. She stared at the red brick wall on the side of the house.
15   Joanna often said softly, "I will not get better."

One afternoon the doctor spoke to Sue. The doctor said, "Joanna is very sick. I am afraid that she may die. Joanna has pneumonia."[1]

1. *pneumonia*: A sickness. A person with pneumonia often has trouble breathing.

Sue was worried. She said, "What can Joanna do to get better?"

The doctor said, "There is something Joanna can do. She must
want to live. She must *want* to get well. She must *believe* she will get
well."

The doctor thought for a moment. Then he said, "What would
Joanna love to do? What is important to her?"

Sue said, "Joanna is an artist. She would love to go to Italy. She
would love to paint the Bay of Naples."

The doctor said, "Joanna should think about that. I will try to
help her get well. I will do everything I can. But she must *want* to
live."

YOU CAN ANSWER THESE QUESTIONS

Put an *x* in the box next to the correct answer.

Reading Comprehension

1. Sue and Joanna loved to
- ❏ **a.** write stories.
- ❏ **b.** go to the movies.
- ❏ **c.** paint.

2. Sue and Joanna were
- ❏ **a.** poor.
- ❏ **b.** rich.
- ❏ **c.** old.

3. Their apartment was
- ❏ **a.** large.
- ❏ **b.** small.
- ❏ **c.** new.

4. Day after day Joanna
- ❏ **a.** ate a lot of food.
- ❏ **b.** stayed in bed.
- ❏ **c.** went to work.

5. Joanna stared at
- ❏ **a.** her friend.
- ❏ **b.** the walls of the apartment.
- ❏ **c.** a red brick wall.

6. The doctor was afraid that Joanna would
- ❏ **a.** leave the apartment.
- ❏ **b.** not pay him.
- ❏ **c.** die.

7. The doctor said it was important for Joanna to
- ❏ **a.** want to live.
- ❏ **b.** get out of bed.
- ❏ **c.** watch TV.

Vocabulary

8. Joanna looked across the alley to the house next door. As used here, the word *alley* means the
- ❏ **a.** floor of a house.
- ❏ **b.** color of a house.
- ❏ **c.** narrow place, or space, between two houses.

9. Joanna got into bed because she felt weak. When you feel *weak*, you
- ❏ **a.** feel strong.
- ❏ **b.** do not feel strong.
- ❏ **c.** feel very good.

Idioms

10. As soon as Joanna got up, she looked at the brick wall. The idiom *as soon as* means
- ❏ **a.** when; just after.
- ❏ **b.** earlier; before.
- ❏ **c.** the next day.

How many questions did you answer correctly? Circle your score. Then fill in your score on the Score Chart on page 168.

Number Correct	1	2	3	4	5	6	7	8	9	10
Score	10	20	30	40	50	60	70	80	90	100

EXERCISES TO HELP YOU

Exercise A

Understanding the story. Answer each question by writing a complete sentence. Begin each sentence with a capital letter. End each sentence with a period. You may use the line numbers in parentheses to find the answers.

1. What kind of apartment did Sue and Joanna live in? (1)

   _____

2. Where is Greenwich Village? (2)

   _____

3. What did Sue and Joanna love to do? (3)

   _____

4. What kind of windows did their apartment have? (7)

   _____

   _____

5. What did Joanna do all day? (10)

   _____

6. What must Joanna believe? (20)

   _____

7. Where did Joanna want to go? (24)

   _____

8. What did Joanna want to paint? (25)

   _____

   _____

Exercise B

Building sentences. Make sentences by adding the correct letter.

1. _____ Many artists   **a.** she felt sick.
2. _____ Their apartment had   **b.** in bed all day.
3. _____ Joanna got into bed because   **c.** beautiful, big windows.
4. _____ She stayed   **d.** are poor.

Now write the sentences on the lines below. Remember to begin each sentence with a capital letter and to end each sentence with a period.

1. _____

2. _____

 _____

3. _____

4. _____

Now do questions 5–8 the same way.

5. _____ Joanna did   **a.** must want to live.
6. _____ She thought she would not   **b.** not eat.
7. _____ Sue was   **c.** very worried about Joanna.
8. _____ The doctor said that Joanna   **d.** get better.

5. _____

6. _____

7. _____

8. _____

 _____

Exercise C

Adding vocabulary. On the left are 7 words and an idiom from the story. Complete each sentence by adding the correct word or words.

apartment

day after day

rent

cough

brick

artists

breathe

moment

1. Sue and Joanna saved their money to pay the _____.

2. They liked the _____ they lived in very much.

3. Many _____ live in Greenwich Village.

4. Joanna began to _____, so she got into bed.

5. It was hard for Joanna to _____ because she had pneumonia.

6. Joanna stayed in bed _____.

7. She stared at the red _____ wall on the side of the house.

8. The doctor thought for a _____ before he spoke.

Exercise D

Changing statements to questions. Change each statement to a question that begins with *What*. Put a question mark at the end of each question. The first one has been done for you.

1. Sue and Joanna were friends.

   What were Sue and Joanna?

2. Joanna and Sue were artists.

   _____

3. Sue and Joanna loved to paint.

   _____

4. Joanna stared out the window all day.

_____

5. Joanna often said, "I will not get better."

_____

6. Joanna wanted to paint the Bay of Naples.

_____

Exercise E

Part A

True or false sentences. Write **T** if the sentence is true. Write **F** if the sentence is false.

1. _____ Sue and Joanna lived in New Jersey.

2. _____ They liked their apartment very much.

3. _____ Joanna got sick in January.

4. _____ Joanna thought she would get better.

5. _____ Joanna ate three meals every day.

6. _____ The doctor said that Joanna was very sick.

Part B

On the lines below, correct the false sentences.

a. _____

b. _____

c. _____

d. _____

Exercise F

Vocabulary review. Write a complete sentence for each word or group of words.

1. alley _____

_____

2. weak _____

_____

3. cough _____

_____

4. brick _____

_____

5. artist _____

_____

6. breathe _____

_____

7. day after day _____

_____

8. as soon as _____

_____

SHARING WITH OTHERS

It is fun to share ideas with others. Discuss these questions with your partner or with the group. Write your answer to one of the questions.

◆ Tell about a time you were sick. How did you get better? If you have never been sick, explain why.

◆ Why was it so important for Joanna to *want* to get well?

_____

_____

_____

_____

_____

PART 2

Later that day Sue went into Joanna's room. Sue took some drawing paper with her. Sue drew beautiful pictures for children's books. She used the money she earned to help pay the rent.

Sue saw Joanna lying on the bed. Joanna's eyes were wide open.
5   She was looking out the window. Joanna was counting. Sue listened.

"*Twelve*," said Joanna. "*Eleven. Ten. Nine.*" Joanna kept staring out the window.

Sue said to herself, "What is Joanna counting?" Sue walked across the room. She looked out the window. She looked across the
10   alley. She saw the red brick wall on the side of the house. She saw a long **vine.** It was climbing up the brick wall.

Once there were many leaves on that vine. But now there were just a few leaves on the vine. The cold winds had blown the leaves away.

15   Joanna spoke again. "*Eight*," she said. "I see only eight leaves."

"Joanna, dear," said Sue. "What are you talking about?"

Joanna turned to Sue. Joanna said, "Three days ago that vine was filled with leaves. But now there are only eight leaves on the vine. Most of the leaves are gone. I watched them fall. It will be
20   winter soon."

Joanna turned toward the window again. "Look," she said. "There goes another leaf. See it **floating** to the ground? Now there are seven. There are seven leaves on the vine."

Sue came near the bed. "Joanna," she asked, "why are you
25   counting the leaves?"

Joanna looked at Sue. Joanna said, "I'm waiting for the last leaf to fall. Then I will go, too."

Sue stared at her friend. "What do you mean?" Sue asked.

Joanna said, "When the last leaf falls, then I will die, too. I have
known that for three days. Didn't the doctor tell you?"

"Don't be silly," said Sue. "Of course you'll get better. I spoke to
the doctor today. He told me that."

Sue said, "**Never mind** the leaves—think about yourself. Think
about what you would like to do. Think about getting well! You must
try to get stronger. I'll bring you some hot soup."

Joanna stared out the window. "I'm not very hungry," she said.
"Look. Another leaf just fell. Now there are six."

Joanna turned to Sue. "No, I don't want any soup," she said. "I
just want to look out the window. I want to see the last leaf fall.
When it falls, I will die, too."

Sue said, "Joanna, please close your eyes. Don't look out the
window. I'm going to draw here at the desk. Don't look at the leaves
until I have finished. Please listen to me."

"Can't you draw in the other room?" Joanna asked.

Sue said, "I like the light from this window."

Sue came near the bed. She pulled the covers over Joanna.
"Remember," said Sue, "don't look at those leaves."

"All right," said Joanna. "But tell me when you are finished. I
want to see the last leaf fall."

Joanna closed her eyes. "I'm tired," she said. "I'm very, very
tired. I want to let go of everything. I want to go sailing down, down,
down, like one of those poor, tired leaves."

YOU CAN ANSWER THESE QUESTIONS

Put an *x* in the box next to the correct answer.

Reading Comprehension

1. Which sentence is true?
   - ❏ **a.** Sue sold children's books.
   - ❏ **b.** Sue drew pictures for children's books.
   - ❏ **c.** Sue wrote children's books.

2. When Sue came into the room, Joanna was
   - ❏ **a.** reading.
   - ❏ **b.** writing.
   - ❏ **c.** counting.

3. There were only a few leaves on the vine because
   - ❏ **a.** people picked the leaves off the vine.
   - ❏ **b.** the vine was very small.
   - ❏ **c.** the wind had blown the leaves away.

4. Joanna said that when the last leaf fell, she would
   - ❏ **a.** feel better.
   - ❏ **b.** get out of bed.
   - ❏ **c.** die.

5. Sue wanted to give Joanna some
   - ❏ **a.** soup.
   - ❏ **b.** milk.
   - ❏ **c.** water.

6. What was Sue going to do at the desk?
   - ❏ **a.** read a book
   - ❏ **b.** write a letter
   - ❏ **c.** draw a picture

7. Joanna was waiting to see
   - ❏ **a.** another doctor.
   - ❏ **b.** a TV show.
   - ❏ **c.** the last leaf fall.

Vocabulary

8. The vine was climbing up the brick wall. A *vine* is a kind of
   - ❏ **a.** bird.
   - ❏ **b.** plant.
   - ❏ **c.** food.

9. A leaf was floating to the ground. As used here, the word *floating* means
   - ❏ **a.** moving slowly in the air.
   - ❏ **b.** burning brightly.
   - ❏ **c.** breaking to pieces.

Idioms

10. Sue told Joanna, "Never mind the leaves—think about yourself." The idiom *never mind* means
   - ❏ **a.** ask about.
   - ❏ **b.** think about.
   - ❏ **c.** don't think about.

How many questions did you answer correctly? Circle your score. Then fill in your score on the Score Chart on page 168.

Number Correct	1	2	3	4	5	6	7	8	9	10
Score	10	20	30	40	50	60	70	80	90	100

Exercise A

Understanding the story. Answer each question by writing a complete sentence. Begin each sentence with a capital letter. End each sentence with a period. You may use the line numbers in parentheses to find the answers.

1. What did Sue take into Joanna's room? (2)

   _____

2. What did Sue draw? (2)

   _____

3. How did Sue use the money she earned? (3)

   _____

   _____

4. When Sue came into the room, what was Joanna doing? (5)

   _____

5. When Sue looked out the window, what did she see? (11)

   _____

6. What was Joanna waiting for? (26)

   _____

7. What did Sue want to give Joanna? (35)

   _____

8. What did Joanna want to see? (39)

   _____

Exercise B

Building sentences. Make sentences by adding the correct letter.

1. _____ Sue saw Joanna   **a.** left on the vine.
2. _____ The vine was climbing   **b.** winter soon.
3. _____ There were only a few leaves   **c.** lying on the bed.
4. _____ It will be   **d.** up the brick wall.

Write the sentences on the lines below. Remember to begin each sentence with a capital letter and to end each sentence with a period.

1. _____

2. _____

3. _____

_____

4. _____

Now do questions 5–8 the same way.

5. _____ Joanna turned toward   **a.** because she was tired.
6. _____ Sue told Joanna to   **b.** not hungry.
7. _____ Joanna said that she was   **c.** the window.
8. _____ She closed her eyes   **d.** think about getting well.

5. _____

6. _____

_____

7. _____

8. _____

_____

Exercise C

Adding vocabulary. On the left are 5 words and an idiom from the story. Complete each sentence by adding the correct word or words.

stronger

draw

desk

leaf

of course

rent

1. Sue said she wanted to work at the _____.

2. She used the money to pay the _____.

3. "Can't you _____ in the other room?" asked Joanna.

4. Sue hoped that Joanna would get _____.

5. Joanna watched another _____ as it fell slowly to the ground.

6. Sue told Joanna, "You'll get better, _____."

Exercise D

Using verbs correctly. Fill in each blank using the **past tense** of the irregular verb in parentheses.

1. Sue _____ some drawing paper into the room. (take)

2. She _____ pictures for children's books. (draw)

3. The cold winds _____ most of the leaves away. (blow)

4. She said, "I _____ to the doctor today." (speak)

5. Later that day Sue _____ into Joanna's room. (go)

Exercise E
Part A
Adding an adjective. Complete the sentences below by adding the correct adjective. Each sentence tells something about the story. Use each adjective once.

long   cold   red   hot   beautiful

1. Sue drew _____ pictures for children's books.

2. The _____ winds had blown the leaves away.

3. Sue looked at the _____ brick wall on the side of the house.

4. A _____ vine was climbing up the wall.

5. Sue wanted to give Joanna some _____ soup.

Part B
Now make up your own sentences using the same adjectives.

1. _____

_____

2. _____

_____

3. _____

_____

4. _____

_____

5. _____

_____

Vocabulary review. Write a complete sentence for each word or group of words.

1. vine _____

_____

2. floating _____

_____

3. leaf _____

_____

4. draw _____

_____

5. of course _____

_____

6. never mind _____

_____

SHARING WITH OTHERS

It is fun to share ideas with others. Discuss these questions with your partner or with the group. Write your answer to one of the questions.

◆ Do you think Joanna will die when the last leaf falls? Why?
◆ Should Sue have tried to make Joanna eat the soup? Why?

_____

_____

_____

_____

_____

PART 3

"Yes," said Joanna, "I'm very, very tired. I want to go sailing down, down, down, like one of those poor, tired leaves."

"Try to sleep," said Sue. "I must go downstairs now. I'm going to ask Mr. Behrman to come up here. I must draw a picture of an old man with a white beard. Mr. Behrman said that I could draw him. I'll be back right away."

Mr. Behrman was an artist who lived in the building. Behrman had been painting for more than forty years. Nobody bought his paintings. But he still dreamed of painting a great picture. He often said, "One day I will paint a great painting. I will paint a great work of art!"

People laughed at Behrman. Then he said, "I'll do it. You'll see." Meanwhile he earned money by driving a **taxi.**

Sue knocked on Behrman's door.

"Come in," he called.

The old man looked at Sue. He saw that she was very unhappy. "What is wrong?" he asked.

Sue told him what Joanna had said.

"What?" said Behrman. "What?" he said again. "She thinks she will die because leaves fall from a vine!" Behrman rubbed his beard. "Why do you let Joanna talk that way?" he asked angrily.

Sue said, "Joanna is very ill. She is weak. She doesn't know what she is saying."

"Poor Joanna," Behrman said. "She is sick. And it is cold in New York."

Behrman thought for a moment. Then his eyes began to **shine.** "Someday I will paint a great painting," he said happily. "I will have plenty of money. Then you and Joanna can take a vacation. You can go to some place where it's warm."

Sue smiled. "Yes, Mr. Behrman," she said. "But now come upstairs with me. I want you to sit in the chair by the window. I want to draw you."

They went upstairs. Sue quietly opened the door. She looked inside. She saw that Joanna was asleep in bed. Sue and Behrman walked to the window. They looked outside. They saw the brick wall. They stared at the vine. Then they looked at each other. There was fear in their eyes.

Suddenly they heard a **tapping** at the window. They looked outside again. It was beginning to rain. Then it began to snow.

Behrman sat down in the chair. Sue began to draw him.

Sue was sleeping the next morning. Suddenly she heard Joanna's voice. Joanna was calling her.

Sue went into Joanna's room. Joanna was in bed. She was staring at the window. The shade was down. It covered the window.

"Raise the shade," said Joanna. "I want to look outside."

Sue was worried, but she slowly pulled up the shade.

It had rained all night. It had snowed **now and then**. Strong winds had blown. But there was one leaf against the brick wall. There still was one leaf! It was the last leaf on the vine.

The leaf was bright green. It had yellow edges. It hung bravely from the vine.

"It's the last leaf," said Joanna. "I'm surprised it's still there. I thought it would fall during the night. I heard the wind. It howled for hours."

Joanna turned to Sue. Joanna said, "I know the leaf will fall today. And I will die at the same time."

"Please don't say that," said Sue. "You must think about getting better."

But Joanna did not answer.

Put an *x* in the box next to the correct answer.

Reading Comprehension

1. Mr. Behrman sold
- ❑ **a.** many of his paintings.
- ❑ **b.** some of his paintings.
- ❑ **c.** none of his paintings.

2. Behrman dreamed of
- ❑ **a.** painting a great picture.
- ❑ **b.** taking a trip.
- ❑ **c.** buying a new car.

3. Sue told Mr. Behrman that she wanted to
- ❑ **a.** borrow money from him.
- ❑ **b.** draw him.
- ❑ **c.** buy one of his paintings.

4. When Behrman and Sue looked out the window, they saw that
- ❑ **a.** the vine was covered with leaves.
- ❑ **b.** the sun was shining.
- ❑ **c.** it was beginning to rain.

5. When Joanna looked out the window, she saw
- ❑ **a.** one leaf.
- ❑ **b.** two leaves.
- ❑ **c.** many leaves.

6. The last leaf was
- ❑ **a.** brown and dying.
- ❑ **b.** bright green.
- ❑ **c.** falling slowly.

Vocabulary

7. When Behrman thought about painting a great picture, his eyes began to shine. When someone's eyes *shine*, they are
- ❑ **a.** closed.
- ❑ **b.** red.
- ❑ **c.** bright.

8. Suddenly they heard the rain tapping at the window. The word *tapping* means
- ❑ **a.** a loud crash.
- ❑ **b.** a light, quick sound.
- ❑ **c.** someone shouting.

9. Mr. Behrman earned money by driving a taxi. A *taxi* is
- ❑ **a.** a car.
- ❑ **b.** a boat.
- ❑ **c.** an airplane.

Idioms

10. It had rained all night and it snowed now and then. The idiom *now and then* means
- ❑ **a.** all the time.
- ❑ **b.** sometimes.
- ❑ **c.** never.

How many questions did you answer correctly? Circle your score. Then fill in your score on the Score Chart on page 168.

Number Correct	1	2	3	4	5	6	7	8	9	10
Score	10	20	30	40	50	60	70	80	90	100

EXERCISES TO HELP YOU

Exercise A

Understanding the story. Answer each question by writing a complete sentence. Begin each sentence with a capital letter. End each sentence with a period. You may use the line numbers in parentheses to find the answers.

1. Where did Mr. Behrman live? (7)

    _____

2. How long had Behrman been painting? (8)

    _____

    _____

3. Who bought Behrman's paintings? (8)

    _____

4. What did Behrman dream of? (9)

    _____

    _____

5. How did Behrman earn money? (13)

    _____

6. Why did Sue want Behrman to sit in the chair by the window? (32)

    _____

7. What color was the last leaf? (50)

    _____

8. Why was Joanna surprised to see the leaf? (53)

    _____

    _____

Exercise B
Building sentences. Make sentences by adding the correct letter.

1. _____ Sue was going to draw a picture of   **a.** very unhappy.
2. _____ Mr. Behrman saw that Sue was   **b.** Joanna was sick.
3. _____ He was sad because   **c.** in a chair by the window.
4. _____ She asked him to sit   **d.** an old man with a beard.

Now write the sentences on the lines below. Remember to begin each sentence with a capital letter and to end each sentence with a period.

1. _____

_____

2. _____

_____

3. _____

4. _____

_____

Now do questions 5–8 the same way.

5. _____ Joanna asked Sue to   **a.** raise the window shade.
6. _____ There still was one leaf   **b.** fall during the night.
7. _____ She thought the leaf would   **c.** about getting better.
8. _____ Sue told Joanna to think   **d.** against the brick wall.

5. _____

_____

6. _____

7. _____

_____

8. _____

Exercise C

Adding vocabulary. On the left are 6 words from the story. Complete each sentence by adding the correct word.

vacation

shade

art

ill

howled

downstairs

1. Mr. Behrman lived _____ from Sue and Joanna.

2. He wanted them to take a _____ in a place that was warm.

3. He hoped to paint a great work of _____ .

4. Joanna was so _____ that she did not know what she was saying.

5. The window _____ was down, so Joanna could not look outside.

6. Strong winds had _____ for hours that night.

Exercise D

Part A

Finding adverbs. Many adverbs (*quickly, loudly*) end in *ly*. Circle the adverbs in the sentences below.

1. Sue quietly opened the door.

2. The leaf hung bravely from the vine.

3. She was worried, but she slowly pulled up the shade.

4. "Why do you let Joanna talk that way?" Mr. Behrman asked angrily.

Part B

Now make up a new sentence with each adverb you circled.

1. _____

2. _____

3. _____

4. _____

Exercise E

Putting words in correct order. Make sentences by putting the words in the correct order. Write each sentence on the line.

1. building / Behrman / lived / the / in / Mr.

_____

2. wall / brick / the / saw / They

_____

3. at / was / She / window / the / staring

_____

4. yellow / had / edges / leaf / The

_____

5. you / want / I / sit / window / to / the / by

_____

Exercise F

Vocabulary review. Write a complete sentence for each word or group of words.

1. taxi _____

_____

2. shine _____

_____

3. tapping _____

_____

4. vacation _____

_____

5. ill _____

_____

6. howled _____

_____

7. downstairs _____

_____

8. now and then _____

_____

Sharing with Others

It is fun to share ideas with others. Discuss these questions with your partner or with the group. Write your answer to one of the questions.

◆ Sue and Mr. Behrman stared at the vine. Then they looked at each other with fear in their eyes. What do you think they saw? Why was there fear in their eyes?
◆ Why was Sue worried when she pulled up the window shade?

_____

_____

_____

_____

_____

_____

PART 4

All day Joanna looked out the window. All day the last leaf hung on to the vine. Evening came. Joanna stared out the window. It was darker now, but she could see the last leaf. It was still there. She saw it clearly against the brick wall.

Sue came into the room at night. She pulled down the window shade. She turned off the light.

Cold winds blew again that night. It rained. Early the next morning, Joanna said, "Raise the shade."

The leaf was still there!

Joanna kept looking at the leaf. She looked at it for a long time.

Suddenly Joanna called out, "I've been thinking, Sue," she said. "I was wrong! I was so very wrong! Something made that last leaf stay."

Joanna kept staring at the leaf. "Yes," she said. "Something made that last leaf stay. It was to show me how foolish I was. It's wrong to want to die. It's foolish and it's wrong!"

Joanna's voice got stronger. "Please bring me some soup. And I'd like some tea. And put some pillows behind my head. I want to sit up."

An hour later Joanna said, "I'd like to go to Italy someday. I'd like to paint the Bay of Naples."

The doctor came by later. He spoke to Sue in the hall of the apartment.

"Joanna is **improving**," he said. "She is getting better. But now I must hurry downstairs. I must see someone named Behrman. He's an artist, I believe. He is old and weak. He has pneumonia, too."

The doctor looked sad. He said, "Mr. Behrman is very, very sick. There is nothing we can do for him now. I must send him to the hospital.[1] He'll be more comfortable there."

1. *hospital:* a place where people who are sick go to get care.

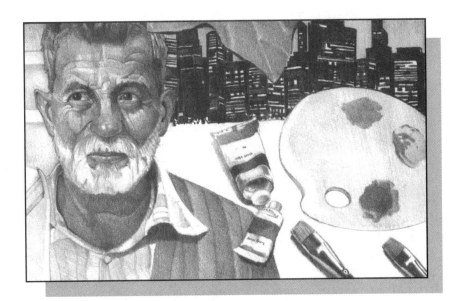

30 The next day the doctor spoke to Sue again. He told her,
"Joanna will get well. She is out of **danger**. She is out of danger
at last. You don't have to worry anymore."

That afternoon Sue sat down at the edge of Joanna's bed. She
looked at Joanna, who was reading a book.
35 "I have something to tell you," Sue said. "Mr. Behrman died
today. He became sick two days ago. That's when he was found in
his room. His clothing and shoes were soaking wet. He was shaking
from the cold.
"Mr. Behrman had been out all night. He had been outside in
40 the rain and the snow. The police found a ladder and his brushes
and his paint in the alley."
Sue stopped. She took a deep breath. Then she said, "Look
out the window, dear. Look at the last leaf on the wall. Didn't you
wonder why it never moved? It didn't even move when the wind
45 blew. Oh, Joanna, it's Behrman's greatest work of art! He painted
the leaf on the brick wall! He painted it there the night that the
last leaf fell."

YOU CAN ANSWER THESE QUESTIONS

Put an *x* in the box next to the correct answer.

Reading Comprehension

1. After the rain, the last leaf
- ❏ **a.** fell to the ground.
- ❏ **b.** broke into pieces.
- ❏ **c.** was still hanging from the vine.

2. Joanna asked Sue for
- ❏ **a.** some soup and some tea.
- ❏ **b.** a glass of milk.
- ❏ **c.** a piece of cake.

3. Joanna wanted to go to Italy to
- ❏ **a.** sit in the sun.
- ❏ **b.** paint the Bay of Naples.
- ❏ **c.** visit some friends.

4. The doctor said that Mr. Behrman was
- ❏ **a.** feeling very well.
- ❏ **b.** very, very sick.
- ❏ **c.** getting better.

5. Mr. Behrman had been sick for
- ❏ **a.** two days.
- ❏ **b.** a week.
- ❏ **c.** two weeks.

6. In the alley, the police found
- ❏ **a.** a letter from Mr. Behrman.
- ❏ **b.** Behrman's brushes and his paint.
- ❏ **c.** Behrman's shoes.

7. The last leaf didn't move because
- ❏ **a.** the wind couldn't reach it.
- ❏ **b.** it was very strong.
- ❏ **c.** it was painted on the wall.

Vocabulary

8. The doctor told Sue that Joanna was improving. When you *improve*, you
- ❏ **a.** get better.
- ❏ **b.** get worse.
- ❏ **c.** stay the same as you were.

9. The doctor said that Joanna was out of danger. The word *danger* means
- ❏ **a.** money.
- ❏ **b.** harm.
- ❏ **c.** food.

Idioms

10. Joanna was getting better at last. The idiom *at last* means
- ❏ **a.** finally.
- ❏ **b.** tomorrow.
- ❏ **c.** next month.

How many questions did you answer correctly? Circle your score. Then fill in your score on the Score Chart on page 168.

Number Correct	1	2	3	4	5	6	7	8	9	10
Score	10	20	30	40	50	60	70	80	90	100

EXERCISES TO HELP YOU

Exercise A

Understanding the story. Answer each question by writing a complete sentence. Begin each sentence with a capital letter. End each sentence with a period. You may use the line numbers in parentheses to find the answers.

1. What did Joanna do all day? (1)

   _____

2. What did Joanna ask for? (17)

   _____

3. Why did Joanna want to go to Italy? (21)

   _____

4. Where was the doctor sending Mr. Behrman? (28)

   _____

5. How long was Mr. Behrman sick? (36)

   _____

6. What did the police find in the alley? (40)

   _____

   _____

7. Where did Mr. Behrman paint the leaf? (46)

   _____

8. When did Mr. Behrman paint the leaf? (46)

   _____

   _____

Exercise B

Building sentences. Make sentences by adding the correct letter.

1. _____ Although it was dark, she   **a.** to sit up.
2. _____ At night Sue pulled down   **b.** Joanna was getting better.
3. _____ Joanna said that she wanted   **c.** could still see the leaf.
4. _____ The doctor told Sue that   **d.** the window shade.

Now write the sentences on the lines below. Remember to begin each sentence with a capital letter and to end each sentence with a period.

1. _____

_____

2. _____

3. _____

4. _____

_____

Now do questions 5–8 the same way.

5. _____ Mr. Behrman had been   **a.** the last leaf fell.
6. _____ He had been outside in   **b.** out all night.
7. _____ The last leaf   **c.** the rain and the snow.
8. _____ Mr. Behrman painted the   **d.** never moved.
leaf after

5. _____

6. _____

_____

7. _____

8. _____

_____

Exercise C

Adding vocabulary. On the left are 5 words and an idiom from the story. Complete each sentence by adding the correct word or words.

foolish

turned off

comfortable

pillows

soaking

ladder

1. At night Sue pulled down the window shade and _____ the light.

2. The doctor thought that Mr. Behrman would be more _____ at the hospital.

3. His clothing and shoes were _____ wet from the rain.

4. Mr. Behrman used a _____ to reach the top of the brick wall.

5. Joanna asked Sue to put some _____ behind her head.

6. Joanna said that it was _____ and wrong to want to die.

Exercise D

Using verbs correctly. Fill in each blank using the **past tense** of the irregular verb in parentheses.

1. The last leaf _____ on to the vine all day. (hang)

2. Joanna said, "Something _____ that last leaf stay there." (make)

3. The police _____ a ladder in the alley. (find)

4. That afternoon Sue _____ down at the edge of Joanna's bed. (sit)

5. Mr. Behrman painted the leaf on the wall after the

   last leaf _____. (fall)

Exercise E

Picking a preposition. Fill in the blanks by adding the correct preposition. Each sentence tells something about the story. Write each preposition once.

for   in   behind   out   to   against

1. All day Joanna looked _____ the window.

2. The police found brushes and paint _____ the alley.

3. Later that day the doctor spoke _____ Sue.

4. Joanna saw the leaf clearly _____ the brick wall.

5. She looked at the leaf _____ a long time.

6. Joanna asked Sue to put some pillows _____ her head.

Exercise F

Vocabulary review. Write a complete sentence for each word or group of words.

1. danger _____

   _____

2. comfortable _____

   _____

3. foolish _____

   _____

4. improving _____

   _____

5. pillow _____

_____

6. ladder _____

_____

7. soaking (wet) _____

_____

8. turned off _____

_____

9. at last _____

_____

SHARING WITH OTHERS

It is fun to share ideas with others. Discuss these questions with your partner or with the group. Write your answer to one of the questions.

◆ Did the story have a happy ending, a sad ending, or both? Why?
◆ What lesson did the last leaf teach Joanna?
◆ O. Henry's stories always end with a surprise. What is the surprise in this story?

_____

_____

_____

_____

_____

_____

_____

_____

THE HERO

by Stephen Crane

THE HERO

by Stephen Crane

This is a war story. It is about the Civil War.

PART 1

The army had been fighting all day. The men were tired. They were hungry and thirsty. Their **uniforms** were covered with earth.

Fred Collins turned to some men nearby. Collins was thirsty. His mouth was dry. Collins said, "I wish I had a drink. Is there any water around here?"

Nobody answered. Then someone yelled, "Look over there! There goes Turner!"

They saw a horse with a soldier on its back. The horse suddenly **rushed** forward. Then something exploded[1] near the horse. The soldier threw up his hands. He tried to cover his face. But it was too late. Smoke filled the air. There were **flames** all around.

The horse fell forward. The soldier fell to the ground. The air was filled with a terrible burning smell.

Collins shook his head and turned away. No one said a word. Everyone was quiet.

Collins looked across the field. He saw grass at the end of the field. He saw an old house that had been hit by shells. The old house was falling down. Only one wall of the house was still standing.

Collins saw a barn. He saw that the roof of the barn was burning. Near the barn was a well.

Collins said, "I wish I had a drink." He turned to a soldier at his side. Collins said, "There's a well up there at the end of the field. I bet there's water in that well."

1. *exploded:* burst or blew up with a loud noise.

25   "Yes," said the soldier. "But how can you get it? You can't go across the field."

      Collins looked at the field again. Shells exploded here and there. Pieces of earth were thrown up in the air. Grass rained down. Bullets flew.

30   "It's getting worse out there," the soldier said.

      A shell struck the old house. There was a loud crash and the last wall fell down. When the smoke cleared, the old house was gone.

      Collins said, "The well is still there. There's water in that well. I sure wish I had a drink."

35   The soldier said, "If you want a drink so much, why don't you go get it?" He laughed. Then another soldier laughed. Soon all the soldiers were laughing.

      Collins got angry when he saw them laughing. "I *will* go!" he said. "I'll go in a minute if you don't **shut up**!"

40   The soldiers laughed again. "You *say* you'll go," a soldier said. "But will you run through that field? Will you run past those bullets?"

      "I'm not afraid to go!" Collins said. "I tell you, I'll go!"

      Then one of the men said, "I dare you to go!"

45   Collins stared at the man and shook his fist. "You'll see!" Collins said. Then he went to find the captain.

Put an *x* in the box next to the correct answer.

Reading Comprehension

1. The army had been fighting
   - ❑ **a.** for just a few minutes.
   - ❑ **b.** for only an hour.
   - ❑ **c.** all day.

2. Which sentence is true?
   - ❑ **a.** The men were not tired.
   - ❑ **b.** The men were not hungry.
   - ❑ **c.** The men were hungry and thirsty.

3. Collins said that he wanted
   - ❑ **a.** a good meal.
   - ❑ **b.** a drink.
   - ❑ **c.** to rest.

4. Near the barn was a
   - ❑ **a.** horse.
   - ❑ **b.** river.
   - ❑ **c.** well.

5. Collins got angry because the soldiers
   - ❑ **a.** laughed at him.
   - ❑ **b.** pushed him.
   - ❑ **c.** began to fight with him.

6. At the end of Part One, Collins
   - ❑ **a.** ran across the field.
   - ❑ **b.** went to find the captain.
   - ❑ **c.** hit one of the soldiers.

Vocabulary

7. The men's uniforms were covered with earth. What are *uniforms*?
   - ❑ **a.** guns
   - ❑ **b.** clothing
   - ❑ **c.** food

8. The horse suddenly rushed forward. The word *rushed* means
   - ❑ **a.** moved quickly.
   - ❑ **b.** turned back.
   - ❑ **c.** stopped.

9. There were flames, and the air was filled with a burning smell. You find *flames* in a
   - ❑ **a.** barn.
   - ❑ **b.** field.
   - ❑ **c.** fire.

Idioms

10. Collins said he would go across the field if the soldiers didn't shut up. The idiom *shut up* means
    - ❑ **a.** be quiet.
    - ❑ **b.** close a door.
    - ❑ **c.** leave for home.

How many questions did you answer correctly? Circle your score. Then fill in your score on the Score Chart on page 168.

Number Correct	1	2	3	4	5	6	7	8	9	10
Score	10	20	30	40	50	60	70	80	90	100

EXERCISES TO HELP YOU

Exercise A

Understanding the story. Answer each question by writing a complete sentence. Begin each sentence with a capital letter. End each sentence with a period. You may use the line numbers in parentheses to find the answers.

1. How long had the army been fighting? (1)

   _____

2. How did the men feel? (1)

   _____

3. What did Fred Collins want? (4)

   _____

4. What happened to the soldier on the horse? (12)

   _____

5. Where was the well? (21)

   _____

6. Why did Collins get angry? (38)

   _____

   _____

7. Who did Collins go to find? (46)

   _____

Exercise B

Building sentences. Make sentences by adding the correct letter.

1. _____ They saw a horse with	**a.** was falling down.
2. _____ The soldier tried	**b.** a soldier on its back.
3. _____ The old house	**c.** and turned away.
4. _____ Fred Collins shook his head	**d.** to cover his face.

Now write the sentences on the lines below. Remember to begin each sentence with a capital letter and to end each sentence with a period.

1. _____

_____

2. _____

3. _____

4. _____

_____

Now do questions 5–8 the same way.

5. _____ Collins thought there was water	**a.** were thrown in the air.
6. _____ Pieces of earth	**b.** afraid to go.
7. _____ All the soldiers	**c.** in the well.
8. _____ Collins said he wasn't	**d.** laughed at Collins.

5. _____

_____

6. _____

7. _____

8. _____

Exercise C

Adding vocabulary. On the left are 6 words from the story. Complete each sentence by adding the correct word.

soldiers

worse

captain

smoke

dared

rushed

1. The air was filled with _____.

2. Soon all the _____ were laughing at Collins.

3. The horse suddenly _____ forward.

4. "It's getting _____ out there," a soldier said.

5. Then one of the men _____ Collins to go.

6. Collins went to find the _____.

Exercise D

Using verbs correctly. Fill in each blank using the **past tense** of the irregular verb in parentheses.

1. The soldier _____ up his hands and tried to cover his face. (throw)

2. Bullets _____ across the field. (fly)

3. Fred Collins said, "I wish I _____ a drink." (have)

4. A shell _____ the old house and the wall fell down. (strike)

5. Collins stared at the man and _____ his fist. (shake)

Exercise E

Picking a preposition. Fill in the blanks by adding the correct preposition. Each sentence tells something about the story. Use each preposition once.

of   with   around   at   by   across

1. The men were covered _____ earth.

2. Collins asked, "Is there any water _____ here?"

3. Collins shook his fist and stared _____ the man.

4. The soldier said, "How can you get the water if you

can't go _____ the field?"

5. The roof _____ the barn was burning.

6. The old house had been hit _____ a shell.

Exercise F

Vocabulary review. Write a complete sentence for each word or group of words.

1. soldier _____

_____

2. captain _____

_____

3. worse _____

_____

4. dare _____

_____

5. rushed _____

_____

6. flames _____

_____

7. uniforms _____

_____

8. shut up _____

_____

SHARING WITH OTHERS

It is fun to share ideas with others. Discuss these questions with your partner or with the group. Write your answer to one of the questions.

◆ Why do you think Fred Collins went to find the captain?
◆ What do you think Collins will say to the captain? What do you think the captain will say to Collins?

_____

_____

_____

_____

_____

_____

PART 2

Collins saluted and said, "Excuse me, Captain."

"Yes?" said the captain.

"Sir," said Collins. "There is water in that well over there." Collins pointed toward the well. "I would like to get some water."

The captain was surprised. He said, "You want water from that well? You must be very thirsty."

"Yes, sir," said Collins.

The captain thought for a moment. Then he said, "Can't you wait?"

"No, sir," Collins said.

The captain looked at Collins. "Son," the captain said, "are you sure you want to do that?"

"Yes, sir," said Collins.

"Think about it," said the captain. "Think about the danger. Are you sure you want to go?"

"I want to go," said Collins.

"Well, then," the captain said, "if you want to go, you can go."

Collins saluted. "Thank you," he said.

Collins walked away. The captain shouted to him, "Collins! Bring back some water for the men . . . and hurry back!"

The captain watched Collins. He saw him talking to the men. A soldier slapped Collins on the back. Some of the men called out, "Good luck."

The captain shook his head. "I guess he's going," the captain said to himself.

Suddenly Collins felt strange. For a moment he thought he was in a dream. But the soldiers were excited. They asked **over and over**, "Are you sure you're going?"

Collins looked at them. "Of course I'm going," he said.

Collins pulled his cap down over his head. He threw back his shoulders. Then he walked quickly away.

Everybody watched. Nobody spoke.

Finally somebody said, "I don't believe it! Look at that! I didn't think he would do it!"

Another soldier asked, "What is Collins doing?"

A soldier answered, "He's going to that well over there. He's going to get some water."

The soldier was surprised. He said, "We're not dying of thirst. He's crazy!"

"Well, somebody dared him to go. Now he's doing it."

Collins stopped at the edge of the field. He looked back at the men. He was all alone. There was danger ahead, but he didn't want to turn back. He said he would do it! Now he *had* to cross the field! He had to face death! Then, suddenly, he didn't feel afraid.

Collins walked thirty feet into the field. He knew that the men were watching him. He looked across the field. Suddenly he saw enemy soldiers. They lifted their **rifles**. They fired. Collins heard the shots. Bullets flew by his head.

Collins ran wildly toward the well. He threw himself down on the ground and began to **crawl**. He crawled closer to the well. At last he was there! He stared into the well. It was dark in the well, but he saw water at the bottom.

Collins took the cap off the water bottle he had brought with him. There was a **cord** at the end of the bottle. Collins held on to the cord. He dropped the bottle into the well. Water flowed slowly into the bottle.

Collins lay there on the ground. Then suddenly he felt very weak. He said to himself, "What am I doing here?" He was filled with fear. He was filled with **terror**. He could not move. He thought, "I'm going to die! I'm dead! I'm dead!"

You Can Answer These Questions

Put an *x* in the box next to the correct answer.

Reading Comprehension

1. Collins told the captain that he wanted to
   - ❏ **a.** go home.
   - ❏ **b.** get some water.
   - ❏ **c.** rest for a while.

2. The captain told Collins to
   - ❏ **a.** stay with the other men.
   - ❏ **b.** leave in an hour.
   - ❏ **c.** hurry back.

3. What did Collins see at the bottom of the well?
   - ❏ **a.** mud
   - ❏ **b.** water
   - ❏ **c.** nothing

4. What did Collins drop into the well?
   - ❏ **a.** a stone
   - ❏ **b.** his cap
   - ❏ **c.** an empty water bottle

5. At the end of Part Two, Collins felt
   - ❏ **a.** afraid.
   - ❏ **b.** happy.
   - ❏ **c.** brave.

Vocabulary

6. The soldiers lifted their rifles and fired. What are *rifles*?
   - ❏ **a.** guns
   - ❏ **b.** hands
   - ❏ **c.** hats

7. He got down and began to crawl. When you *crawl*, you move
   - ❏ **a.** as fast as you can.
   - ❏ **b.** up and down.
   - ❏ **c.** on your hands and knees.

8. Collins held on to the cord at the end of the bottle. A *cord* is a
   - ❏ **a.** piece of rope.
   - ❏ **b.** piece of paper.
   - ❏ **c.** piece of glass.

9. Collins could not move because he was filled with terror. The word *terror* means
   - ❏ **a.** much food.
   - ❏ **b.** much fear.
   - ❏ **c.** much joy.

Idioms

10. The soldiers asked over and over, "Are you going?" The idiom *over and over* means
    - ❏ **a.** high above.
    - ❏ **b.** very softly.
    - ❏ **c.** again and again.

How many questions did you answer correctly? Circle your score. Then fill in your score on the Score Chart on page 168.

Number Correct	1	2	3	4	5	6	7	8	9	10
Score	10	20	30	40	50	60	70	80	90	100

Exercise A

Understanding the story. Answer each question by writing a complete sentence. Begin each sentence with a capital letter. End each sentence with a period. You may use the line numbers in parentheses to find the answers.

1. What did Collins want to get? (4)

   _____

2. What did the captain tell Collins to bring back? (20)

   _____

   _____

3. Why didn't Collins want to turn back? (43)

   _____

4. What did he see at the bottom of the well? (52)

   _____

5. What did Collins take off the water bottle? (53)

   _____

6. What did he drop into the well? (55)

   _____

7. What did Collins ask himself? (58)

   _____

   _____

8. What did he think would happen to him? (60)

   _____

Exercise B

Building sentences. Make sentences by adding the correct letter.

1. _____ Collins said there was	**a.**	walked quickly away.
2. _____ The captain asked Collins to	**b.**	water in the well.
3. _____ For a moment Collins thought he	**c.**	think about the danger.
4. _____ He pulled down his cap and	**d.**	was in a dream.

Now write the sentences on the lines below. Remember to begin each sentence with a capital letter and to end each sentence with a period.

1. _____

2. _____

   _____

3. _____

   _____

4. _____

   _____

Now do questions 5–8 the same way.

5. _____ Collins walked thirty feet	**a.**	very weak.
6. _____ He knew that the men	**b.**	himself down on the ground.
7. _____ He ran wildly toward the well and threw	**c.**	were watching him.
8. _____ Then suddenly he felt	**d.**	into the field.

5. _____

6. _____

7. _____

   _____

8. _____

Exercise C

Adding vocabulary. On the left are 6 words from the story. Complete each sentence by adding the correct word.

crazy

slapped

saluted

edge

thirst

enemy

1. When he saw the captain, Collins _____.

2. A soldier _____ Collins on the back.

3. Collins stopped at the _____ of the field.

4. A soldier thought that Collins was _____ to go to the well.

5. Suddenly he saw the _____ soldiers in the distance.

6. Someone said, "We're not dying of _____.

Exercise D

Part A

Using verbs correctly. Fill in each blank in the paragraph by writing the **future tense** of the verb in parentheses. Use *will* plus the verb. The first one has been done for you.

Fred Collins thought to himself, "I ___*will go*___ (go) across the
1

field. I _____ (get) some water from the well. Then I
2

_____ (bring) the water back to the men. Everybody
3

_____ (drink) the water. Then they _____ (feel) much
4   5

better."

Part B

On the lines below write sentences using the future tense of these verbs.

speak   work   call   write

1. _____

2. _____

3. _____

4. _____

Exercise E
Part A

Changing adjectives to adverbs. Change adjectives to adverbs by adding *ly*. Complete the sentence by writing in the correct adverb. The first one has been done for you.

1. The captain spoke to Collins in a loud voice. The captain

    spoke ___*loudly*___ .

2. Collins answered in a soft voice. Collins spoke _____ .

3. Some soldiers thought that Collins was a brave man.

    He acted _____ .

4. Collins moved in a very quiet way. He moved _____ .

5. Will this story have a sad ending? Will it end _____ ?

Part B
Add *ly* to the following adjectives to make adverbs. Use each adverb in a sentence.

   slow   quick   neat   nice   careful

1. _____

2. _____

3. _____

4. _____

5. _____

Exercise F
Vocabulary review. Write a complete sentence for each word or group of words.

1. slapped _____

    _____

2. crazy _____

    _____

3. enemy _____

_____

4. thirst _____

_____

5. saluted _____

_____

6. rifles _____

_____

7. crawl _____

_____

8. cord _____

_____

9. terror _____

_____

10. over and over _____

_____

SHARING WITH OTHERS

It is fun to share ideas with others. Discuss these questions with your partner or with the group. Write your answer to one of the questions.

◆ Suppose you were the captain. Would you have let Collins go to the well? Why?

◆ A soldier said that Collins was crazy. Do you think Collins was crazy, brave, or foolish? Why?

_____

_____

_____

_____

PART 3

Collins took a deep breath. Then he looked down into the well. He saw that the bottle was half full. He began to feel a little stronger.

Suddenly something exploded near him. Collins saw a flash of fire and then flames and smoke. He quickly pulled up the bottle.

5　　Collins jumped up and looked around. He didn't know what to do. Then he saw a wooden **bucket** on the ground. It was the bucket for the well.

Collins grabbed the bucket by its chain. He **lowered** the bucket into the well. When the bucket was full, he pulled it up.

10　　Collins held the bucket of water and began to run. He ran as fast as he could. He was filled with fear. He was afraid that a bullet would hit him. He was afraid that he would be shot dead.

Collins ran past a **wounded** man. "Young man," the soldier called. "Give me a drink of water, please."

15　　Collins was afraid to stop. "I can't!" he screamed.

Collins kept running. His cap fell off. His hair flew wildly.

Then Collins stopped running. He turned and ran back to the wounded man.

"Here's your drink!" Collins yelled. "Here it is! Here it is!"

20　　But the man could not lift his arm to take the water. He was falling slowly to the ground.

Collins grabbed the wounded soldier. "Here it is!" Collins said. "Here's your drink! Take it, man!"

The man did not move.

25　　"I'll help you," Collins said. But Collins's hands were shaking. He could not keep the bucket from moving. Water splashed all over the face of the dying man.

Collins pulled the bucket away. Then he began to run again.

A few minutes later Collins was back with the men. When they saw him they cheered.

Collins offered the bucket of water to the captain.

"No," the captain said. "Let the men drink first."

Two young soldiers were the first to get the bucket. They were very happy and began to **fool around**. When one soldier tried to drink, the other soldier pulled his arm.

"Don't do that," said the first man. "You'll make me spill the water."

The other man laughed. He pulled his friend's arm again.

Suddenly there was a loud yell. The bucket crashed to the ground! Everyone was shocked! The two soldiers stared at each other. The bucket was lying on the ground—empty.

You Can Answer These Questions

Put an *x* in the box next to the correct answer.

Reading Comprehension

1. When Collins looked into the well, he saw that the bottle was
   - ❏ **a.** empty.
   - ❏ **b.** half full.
   - ❏ **c.** full.

2. Collins was afraid that he would
   - ❏ **a.** fall down.
   - ❏ **b.** lose his cap.
   - ❏ **c.** be shot.

3. The wounded soldier asked for
   - ❏ **a.** some food.
   - ❏ **b.** warm clothing.
   - ❏ **c.** a drink of water.

4. Which sentence is true?
   - ❏ **a.** Collins splashed water all over the face of the dying man.
   - ❏ **b.** The dying man lifted the bucket to his mouth.
   - ❏ **c.** The dying man took a long drink.

5. The captain told Collins to
   - ❏ **a.** take the first drink.
   - ❏ **b.** be careful not to spill the water.
   - ❏ **c.** let the men drink first.

6. At the end of the story,
   - ❏ **a.** the bucket fell to the ground.
   - ❏ **b.** the captain drank from the bucket.
   - ❏ **c.** all the soldiers drank from the bucket.

Vocabulary

7. Collins saw the wooden bucket for the well. A *bucket* is
   - ❏ **a.** a large hammer.
   - ❏ **b.** a pail for carrying things.
   - ❏ **c.** a heavy box.

8. Collins lowered the bucket into the well. The word *lowered* means
   - ❏ **a.** broke.
   - ❏ **b.** pulled.
   - ❏ **c.** let down.

9. The wounded soldier fell down. The word *wounded* means
   - ❏ **a.** hurt.
   - ❏ **b.** old.
   - ❏ **c.** tall.

Idioms

10. The two soldiers were happy and began to fool around. The idiom *fool around* means
    - ❏ **a.** to play and joke.
    - ❏ **b.** to be sorry.
    - ❏ **c.** to be angry.

How many questions did you answer correctly? Circle your score. Then fill in your score on the Score Chart on page 168.

Number Correct	1	2	3	4	5	6	7	8	9	10
Score	10	20	30	40	50	60	70	80	90	100

EXERCISES TO HELP YOU

Exercise A

Understanding the story. Answer each question by writing a complete sentence. Begin each sentence with a capital letter. End each sentence with a period. You may use the line numbers in parentheses to find the answers.

1. What did Collins see on the ground? (6)

_____

2. When did Collins pull up the bucket? (9)

_____

3. What was Collins afraid of? (12)

_____

_____

4. What did the wounded man ask for? (14)

_____

5. Why couldn't the wounded man take the water? (20)

_____

_____

6. What did the men do when they saw Collins? (30)

_____

7. Who got the bucket first? (33)

_____

_____

8. What happened to the bucket? (39)

_____

Exercise B

Building sentences. Make sentences by adding the correct letter.

1. _____ Collins looked down   **a.** back to the wounded man.
2. _____ When the bucket was   **b.** into the well.
   full, he
3. _____ Collins's cap fell off and   **c.** pulled it up.
4. _____ He turned and ran   **d.** his hair flew wildly.

Now write the sentences on the lines below. Remember to begin each sentence with a capital letter and to end each sentence with a period.

1. _____

2. _____

3. _____

4. _____

_____

Now do questions 5–8 the same way.

5. _____ The man could not lift his   **a.** the other soldier pulled
   arm   his arm.
6. _____ A few minutes later Collins   **b.** to take the water.
7. _____ When one soldier tried   **c.** stared at each other.
   to drink,
8. _____ The two soldiers   **d.** was back with the men.

5. _____

_____

6. _____

_____

7. _____

_____

8. _____

Exercise C

Adding vocabulary. On the left are 6 words from the story. Complete each sentence by adding the correct word.

splashed

chain

cheered

offered

flash

spill

1. Collins saw a _____ of fire and then flames and smoke.

2. There was a _____ hanging from the bucket.

3. Water _____ all over the face of the dying man.

4. When the men saw Collins they _____.

5. When he got back, Collins _____ the bucket of water to the captain.

6. "You'll make me _____ the water," the soldier said.

Exercise D

Changing statements to questions. Change each statement to a question that begins with *How.* Put a question mark at the end of each question. The first one has been done for you.

1. The bottle was half full.

   How much water was in the bottle? or How full was the bottle?

2. Collins began to feel a little better.

   _____

3. Collins grabbed the bucket by its chain.

   _____

4. He ran as fast as he could.

   _____

5. The two young soldiers were very happy.

   _____

Exercise E

Putting words in correct order. Make sentences by putting the words in the correct order. Write each sentence on the line.

1. began / feel / to / stronger / Collins

    _____.

2. afraid / was / stop / He / running / to

    _____.

3. man / lift / not / arm / his / The / could

    _____.

4. bucket / Collins / the / away / pulled

    _____.

5. ground / lying / on / was / the / bucket / The

    _____.

Exercise F

Vocabulary review. Write a complete sentence for each word or group of words.

1. chain _____

   _____

2. splashed _____

   _____

3. cheered _____

   _____

4. offered _____

   _____

5. spill _____

_____

6. bucket _____

_____

7. lowered _____

_____

8. wounded _____

_____

9. fool around _____

_____

SHARING WITH OTHERS

It is fun to share ideas with others. Discuss these questions with your partner or with the group. Write your answer to one of the questions.

◆ Do you think Collins should have stopped for the dying man? Why?
◆ The story ends with the bucket on the ground—empty. Why do you think the writer ended the story this way? What is he telling the reader?

_____

_____

_____

_____

_____

_____

LAND

by Leo Tolstoy

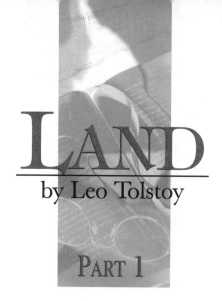

LAND
by Leo Tolstoy

PART 1

Pakhom was a poor farmer, but he dreamed of having much land. Pakhom's farm was very small. It was less than an **acre.** Every morning Pakhom got up early and worked until it was dark. In this way he was able to save some money. Pakhom worked and saved, and he dreamed of having much land.

One day a traveler stopped at Pakhom's farm. The traveler needed food for his horse. Pakhom gave the horse some oats. Then Pakhom and the man drank tea and talked.

The man said, "I am returning from a land that is far away. It is in the south of Russia. It is called the Land of the Bashkirs."

The man told Pakhom that he had bought a piece of land from the Bashkirs. It was a very large piece of land—more than 1,500 acres. The land was **cheap.** It was very cheap. It cost only 500 rubles.

Pakhom was interested in what the traveler said.

The man said, "The Bashkirs are very stupid. They will sell you land for very little money. All you need to do is make friends with them. You must make friends with their Chief."

The man drank some more tea. He said, "It is easy to make friends with the Bashkirs. Give them some gifts. Then they will be your friends." He smiled. "I gave them some tea and some presents. This made them happy. Then they sold me a large piece of land for almost nothing."

The man told Pakhom, "Their land is very good, too. It is near a river. The earth is very rich. You can grow almost anything there."

"Do the Bashkirs own much land?" asked Pakhom.

The traveler laughed. "Oh, yes," he said. "They own many acres. They own more land than you have ever seen. If you walked all year, you could not walk from one end of their land to the other."

Pakhom shook his head and thought about the land.

"I tell you," said the traveler, "the Bashkirs are as stupid as sheep. Just give them some gifts. Then they will sell their land for very little money. They are a happy people who live in tents near the side of a river."

35   Pakhom was **delighted.** He thought, "I must visit the Bashkirs. I have always dreamed of having much land. This may be my chance."

Pakhom asked, "How do you get to the Land of the Bashkirs?"

The traveler told him. Then Pakhom and the man shook hands
40   and the traveler left.

Pakhom told his wife about the Bashkirs. Then Pakhom said, "I will go to see the Bashkirs. I will leave in the morning. You must stay here to **take care of** the farm."

The next day Pakhom and his helper started on their journey.
45   The helper was a strong man. He pulled a heavy wooden **cart**. First they stopped at a town along the way. Pakhom bought some presents and two boxes of tea. The men put everything into the cart.

They traveled for a week. On the seventh day, they saw some tents near the side of a river. It was just as the traveler had said. The

50 Bashkirs lived in the tents. They looked like happy people.

When the Bashkirs saw Pakhom, they came out of their tents. They stood around the visitor. The Bashkirs seemed very happy to see Pakhom. They led him into one of the best tents. They offered him a seat. They sat down around him. They gave him some tea and 55 some food to eat.

Then Pakhom took the presents out of the cart. He gave them to the Bashkirs. He also gave everyone some tea. The Bashkirs were very happy.

Then one of the Bashkirs stepped forward. He told Pakhom, "We 60 like you very much. You gave us presents. We would like to give you something. What can we give you? What do you want?"

"What I like," said Pakhom, "is your land. Our land is not very good. But you have plenty of land, and it is good land. I never saw land as good as this. I would like to buy a piece of your land."

65 The Bashkirs talked to each other. They joked and laughed. Then they were silent. The man stepped forward again.

He said, "We will gladly sell you some land. But we must wait until the Chief returns. We must ask the Chief before we can sell you the land."

YOU CAN ANSWER THESE QUESTIONS

Put an *x* in the box next to the correct answer.

Reading Comprehension

1. The traveler stopped at Pakhom's farm to
- ❏ **a.** rest there for the night.
- ❏ **b.** get food for his horse.
- ❏ **c.** buy another horse.

2. The traveler said that the Bashkirs lived in
- ❏ **a.** small houses.
- ❏ **b.** large buildings.
- ❏ **c.** tents.

3. Pakhom and his helper traveled for
- ❏ **a.** a week.
- ❏ **b.** ten days.
- ❏ **c.** a month.

4. What did Pakhom give the Bashkirs?
- ❏ **a.** tea and presents
- ❏ **b.** money and clothes
- ❏ **c.** food and horses

5. Pakhom told the Bashkirs that he wanted to
- ❏ **a.** stay with them for a week.
- ❏ **b.** buy a piece of land.
- ❏ **c.** teach them about farming.

Vocabulary

6. Pakhom's small farm was less than an acre. The word *acre* means the number of
- ❏ **a.** cows on a farm.
- ❏ **b.** people in a village.
- ❏ **c.** feet in a piece of land.

7. He paid very little. The land was cheap. Something that is *cheap*
- ❏ **a.** costs little.
- ❏ **b.** costs much.
- ❏ **c.** looks pretty.

8. Pakhom was delighted to buy much land for very little money.
The word *delighted* means
- ❏ **a.** very sad.
- ❏ **b.** very happy.
- ❏ **c.** very slow.

9. The men put everything into a wooden cart. What is a *cart*?
- ❏ **a.** a kind of house
- ❏ **b.** a kind of boat
- ❏ **c.** a kind of wagon

Idioms

10. Pakhom's wife stayed at home to take care of the farm. The idiom *take care of* means to
- ❏ **a.** leave.
- ❏ **b.** watch.
- ❏ **c.** buy.

How many questions did you answer correctly? Circle your score. Then fill in your score on the Score Chart on page 168.

Number Correct	1	2	3	4	5	6	7	8	9	10
Score	10	20	30	40	50	60	70	80	90	100

Exercise A

Understanding the story. Answer each question by writing a complete sentence. Begin each sentence with a capital letter. End each sentence with a period. You may use the line numbers in parentheses to find the answers.

1. Who was Pakhom? (1)

_____

2. What did Pakhom dream of having? (1)

_____

3. Why did a traveler stop at Pakhom's farm? (7)

_____

4. What did Pakhom and the traveler drink? (8)

_____

5. Where is the Land of the Bashkirs? (10)

_____

6. How much land did the Bashkirs own? (27)

_____

7. What did Pakhom buy in town? (47)

_____

_____

8. What did Pakhom give the Bashkirs? (56)

_____

9. What did Pakhom want to buy? (64)

_____

10. Who were the Bashkirs waiting for? (68)

_____

Exercise B

Building sentences. Make sentences by adding the correct letter.

1. _____ One day a traveler stopped		**a.**	a large piece of land.
2. _____ The traveler was coming back		**b.**	at Pakhom's farm.
3. _____ The traveler bought		**c.**	almost nothing.
4. _____ He said that the land cost		**d.**	from the Land of the Bashkirs.
5. _____ Pakhom told his wife		**e.**	about the Bashkirs.

Now write the sentences on the lines below. Remember to begin each sentence with a capital letter and to end each sentence with a period.

1. _____

2. _____

_____

3. _____

4. _____

5. _____

Now do questions 6–10 the same way.

6. _____ Pakhom and his helper went		**a.**	their Chief.
7. _____ The helper pulled		**b.**	happy people.
8. _____ The Bashkirs seemed to be		**c.**	to find the Bashkirs.
9. _____ The Bashkirs gave Pakhom		**d.**	a heavy wooden cart.
10. _____ The Bashkirs were waiting for		**e.**	some food to eat.

6. _____

_____

7. _____

8. _____

9. _____

10. _____

Exercise C

Adding vocabulary. On the left are 6 words from the story. Complete each sentence by adding the correct word.

gifts

stupid

own

rubles

oats

seventh

1. Pakhom gave the horse some _____.

2. The traveler thought that the Bashkirs were _____ because they sold land for very little money.

3. The traveler bought the land for 500 _____.

4. Pakhom bought some _____ to give to the Bashkirs.

5. On the _____ day, they saw some tents near the river.

6. Pakhom asked, "Do the Bashkirs _____ much land?"

Exercise D

Writing verbs correctly. Fill in each blank by adding the **past tense** of the regular (1–5) or irregular (6–10) verb in parentheses.

1. Pakhom _____ of having much land. (dream)

2. One day a traveler _____ at Pakhom's farm. (stop)

3. The Bashkirs were a happy people who _____ in tents. (live)

4. They _____ Pakhom some food and tea. (offer)

5. The Bashkirs _____ to each other about Pakhom. (talk)

6. Pakhom and the traveler _____ some tea. (drink)

7. The traveler _____ a large piece of land from the Bashkirs. (buy)

8. The Bashkirs _____ their land for very little money. (sell)

9. The Bashkirs _____ Pakhom into one of their best tents. (lead)

10. The Bashkirs liked Pakhom because he _____ them presents. (give)

Exercise E

Picking a pronoun. Fill in the blanks by adding the correct **object pronoun**. Each sentence tells something about the story. Use each pronoun once.

me	us
you	you
her, him, it	them

1. The traveler saw the Bashkirs and gave _____ some tea.

2. The traveler said, "Their land is so good, you can grow anything on

   _____."

3. They will sell you land if their Chief likes_____ .

4. He said, "They sold _____ a large piece of land for

   almost nothing."

5. When the Bashkirs saw Pakhom, they stood around _____.

6. Pakhom told the Bashkirs, "Let me give _____ some gifts."

7. The Bashkirs said, "We like you very much because you

   gave _____ presents."

8. Pakhom spoke to his wife and told _____ about the Bashkirs.

Exercise F

Vocabulary review. Write a complete sentence for each word or group of words.

1. gifts _____

   _____

2. oats _____

   _____

3. own _____

_____

4. stupid _____

_____

5. seventh _____

_____

6. acre _____

_____

7. cheap _____

_____

8. delighted _____

_____

9. cart _____

_____

10. take care of _____

_____

SHARING WITH OTHERS

It is fun to share ideas with others. Discuss these questions with your partner or with the group. Write your answer to one of the questions.

◆ Will the Chief sell Pakhom some land? Why? If you say yes, will the Chief ask for much money? Explain.

◆ Do you think this story will have a happy ending or a sad ending? Why?

_____

_____

_____

_____

PART 2

Just then a tall man arrived. He was wearing a large fur hat and a large fur coat.

"This is our Chief," said one of the Bashkirs.

Pakhom went to the cart at once. He took out a beautiful coat
5   and five pounds of tea. He gave these to the Chief. The Chief took them and sat down. Some of the Bashkirs came near him and **whispered** in his ear.

The Chief listened. Then he said, "I agree."

The Chief turned to Pakhom and said, "Choose whatever piece
10   of land you like. We will sell it to you. We have plenty of land."

"What is the **price**?" asked Pakhom.

"Our price is always the same," said the Chief. "The price is 500 rubles a day."

Pakhom did not understand. He said, "How can the price be
15   500 rubles a day?"

The Chief laughed. "It is easy," he said. "We sell the land by the day. You can have all the land that you can walk around in a day. The price is 500 rubles."

Pakhom was surprised. He could walk around a large piece of
20   land in a day. And 500 rubles was not too much money. He had 500 rubles in his pocket.

Pakhom said, "But in a day I can walk around a very large piece of land."

The Chief laughed. He said, "Then it will be yours!"

25   The Chief stopped laughing. "But there is one thing," he said. "You must return to the place you started. You must return there before the day is over. If you take longer than a day, you lose your money."

"But how will you know where I have walked?" asked Pakhom.

30   "That is easy," said the Chief. "Here is a shovel. Take it with you.

Start at any place you like. As you walk along, dig some holes. They will tell us where you walked."

Pakhom was very happy. He said that he would leave the next morning.

35   That night Pakhom could not sleep. He kept thinking about the land.

He thought, "I will walk around a very large piece of land. I can walk thirty or thirty-five miles in a day. I will have a huge piece of land! I'll sell some of the land, and I'll rent some of it to farmers. But 40   I'll keep the best land for myself! That's where I'll have my farm."

Pakhom thought about the land all night. He finally fell asleep just before dawn. As soon as he closed his eyes, Pakhom had a dream. He dreamed that he was lying in his tent and that he heard someone laughing outside. He dreamed that he went outside and 45   saw the Bashkir Chief. The Chief was laughing loudly.

In his dream Pakhom asked the Chief, "Why are you laughing?" But the Chief did not answer. Pakhom looked closely at the Chief. Then Pakhom saw that it was not the Chief who was laughing. It was the traveler who had told him about the land. The traveler was 50   laughing loudly. The laughter grew louder and louder and louder. Pakhom suddenly woke up.

"That was a strange dream," Pakhom thought to himself.

He looked around and saw that it was early in the morning. "It's time to wake up my helper," he thought. "We must leave now."

⁵⁵ He got up and went outside. He woke up the helper, who was sleeping in the cart. Then he went to call the Bashkirs.

"It's time to go for the land," Pakhom said.

The Bashkirs were ready, and they started to walk. Pakhom carried the shovel in his hand.

⁶⁰ They walked until they came to the top of a hill. Then the Chief came up to Pakhom. The Chief pointed to the plain below. "Look down there," said the Chief. "Everything you can see is ours. You may have whatever land you want."

Pakhom was very happy. He could see that it was wonderful ⁶⁵ land.

The Chief took off his fur hat. He put it on the ground. "This will be the starting point," he said. "Right here." He touched the hat with his foot.

"This is where you will start," said the Chief. "And this is where ⁷⁰ you must finish. Walk wherever you like. All the land that you walk around in a day will be yours. But **keep in mind**, you must return to this spot before the sun sets!"

Pakhom took out his 500 rubles. He put them on the hat.

Then the helper walked toward Pakhom. He gave Pakhom some ⁷⁵ bread and some water. Pakhom put the bread into the pocket of his pants. He pushed the bottle of water inside his belt. He was ready to start.

Put an *x* in the box next to the correct answer.

Reading Comprehension

1. What did Pakhom give the Chief?
   - ❑ **a.** a coat and five pounds of tea
   - ❑ **b.** a wooden cart
   - ❑ **c.** 200 rubles

2. The Chief said that Pakhom could have
   - ❑ **a.** a small piece of land.
   - ❑ **b.** all the land that the Chief owned.
   - ❑ **c.** all the land that Pakhom could walk around in a day.

3. The Chief told Pakhom to
   - ❑ **a.** walk as fast as he could.
   - ❑ **b.** walk very slowly.
   - ❑ **c.** dig some holes as he walked.

4. Pakhom dreamed that the traveler was
   - ❑ **a.** riding a horse.
   - ❑ **b.** talking to the Chief.
   - ❑ **c.** laughing loudly.

5. How far did Pakhom think he could walk in a day?
   - ❑ **a.** about 10 miles
   - ❑ **b.** 30 or 35 miles
   - ❑ **c.** 100 miles

6. Pakhom put the 500 rubles
   - ❑ **a.** under a stone.
   - ❑ **b.** on the Chief's hat.
   - ❑ **c.** next to a tree.

7. The helper gave Pakhom
   - ❑ **a.** money.
   - ❑ **b.** bread and water.
   - ❑ **c.** a bottle filled with tea.

Vocabulary

8. Some of the men came near the Chief and whispered in his ear. When you *whisper,* you
   - ❑ **a.** shout very loudly.
   - ❑ **b.** speak very softly.
   - ❑ **c.** watch very closely.

9. The price of the land was 500 rubles a day. The word *price* means
   - ❑ **a.** cost.
   - ❑ **b.** size.
   - ❑ **c.** color.

Idioms

10. The Chief said, "But keep in mind, you must return to this spot before the sun sets!" The idiom *keep in mind* means
    - ❑ **a.** do not forget.
    - ❑ **b.** ask many questions.
    - ❑ **c.** read a book.

How many questions did you answer correctly? Circle your score. Then fill in your score on the Score Chart on page 168.

Number Correct	1	2	3	4	5	6	7	8	9	10
Score	10	20	30	40	50	60	70	80	90	100

Exercise A

Understanding the story. Answer each question by writing a complete sentence. Begin each sentence with a capital letter. End each sentence with a period. You may use the line numbers in parentheses to find the answers.

1. What was the Chief wearing? (1)

   _____

   _____

2. What did Pakhom give the Chief? (4)

   _____

3. What was the price of the land? (13)

   _____

4. What did the Chief give Pakhom? (30)

   _____

5. Why couldn't Pakhom sleep that night? (35)

   _____

   _____

6. When did Pakhom finally fall asleep? (42)

   _____

   _____

7. What did the Chief put on the ground? (66)

   _____

8. What did the helper give Pakhom? (75)

   _____

   _____

Exercise B

Building sentences. Make sentences by adding the correct letter. Each sentence tells something about the story.

1. _____ Pakhom gave some presents   **a.** choose a piece of land.
2. _____ The Chief said Pakhom could   **b.** a huge piece of land.
3. _____ Pakhom could have all the   **c.** a strange dream.
   land that he
4. _____ Pakhom thought he   **d.** walked around in a day.
   would get
5. _____ That night Pakhom had   **e.** to the Chief.

Now write the sentences on the lines below. Remember to begin each sentence with a capital letter and to end each sentence with a period.

1. _____

2. _____

   _____

3. _____

   _____

4. _____

5. _____

Now do questions 6–10 the same way.

6. _____ The next morning Pakhom   **a.** he wanted to go.
7. _____ They walked until they came   **b.** wonderful land.
8. _____ The Bashkirs had   **c.** to the top of a hill.
9. _____ Pakhom could walk wherever   **d.** the sun set.
10. _____ He had to return before   **e.** woke up his helper.

6. _____

7. _____

8. _____

9. _____

10. _____

Exercise C

Adding vocabulary. On the left are 5 words and an idiom from the story. Complete each sentence by adding the correct word or words.

at once

rent

shovel

pocket

fur

agree

1. The Chief was wearing a large _____ coat.

2. When the Chief arrived, Pakhom went to the cart _____.

3. The Chief said, "I _____ to sell the land to Pakhom."

4. Pakhom had 500 rubles in his _____.

5. The Chief gave Pakhom a _____ so that he could dig some holes.

6. He thought he would sell some of the land and _____ some of it to farmers.

Exercise D

Picking a possessive. Fill in each blank by adding the correct **possessive.** Use each possessive once.

my   yours   his   its   our   their

1. The Chief touched the hat with _____ foot.

2. He said, "Whatever land you walk around will be _____."

3. Pakhom thought, "I'll keep the best land for myself. That's where

   I'll have _____ farm."

4. The man told Pakhom, "This is _____ Chief."

5. Pakhom carried the shovel by _____ handle.

6. The Bashkirs always listened to _____ Chief.

Exercise E

Putting words in correct order. Make sentences by putting the words in the correct order.

1. price / The / was / 500 / day / a / rubles

   _____.

2. sleep / not / night / could / Pakhom / That

   _____.

3. had / Pakhom / dream / strange / a

   _____.

4. Chief / hat / fur / off / took / The / his

   _____.

5. ground / the / He / on / put / hat / the

   _____.

Exercise F

Vocabulary review. Write a complete sentence for each word or group of words.

1. fur _____

   _____

2. pocket _____

   _____

3. shovel _____

   _____

4. rent _____

   _____

5. agree _____

_____

6. whispered _____

_____

7. price _____

_____

8. keep in mind _____

_____

SHARING WITH OTHERS

It is fun to share ideas with others. Discuss these questions with your partner or with the group. Write your answer to one of the questions.

◆ In Pakhom's dream the Chief and the traveler laughed at him. What do you think this means?
◆ How much land do you think Pakhom will walk around? Why?
◆ If you were Pakhom, what would you do?

_____

_____

_____

_____

_____

PART 3

Pakhom looked around. He wondered where to walk. The land was good everywhere.

Finally he thought, "I will walk toward the east." He turned toward the east and waited for the sun to rise.

Soon Pakhom saw the first light of the sun. He walked down the hill and marched on to the plain.

Pakhom walked quickly. He carried the shovel over his shoulder. After he had walked about a mile, Pakhom stopped. "This is where I will dig the first hole," he thought. Pakhom dug the hole and put the little pile of earth next to it. "That will make the hole easier to see," he said. He walked on for a while. Then he dug another hole.

Pakhom looked back. He could see the hill with the people on it. He guessed that he had walked three miles. It was getting warmer. He took off his coat and threw it over his shoulder. Then he walked until he stopped to dig another hole.

It was getting very warm. Pakhom looked at the sun and felt a little tired. "I will take off my heavy boots," he said. "That will make it easier to walk." Pakhom sat down and took off his boots. Then he stood up and began to walk. It was easier to walk without his boots.

"I will walk for another three miles," he thought. "Then I will turn to the left. The land here is very good. I don't want to give it up."

Pakhom walked for a long time. Then he turned around and looked toward the hill. It was far away. The people on the hill looked very small.

Pakhom thought, "I have gone far enough in this direction. I must stop here and turn to the left. Anyway, I am very thirsty."

Pakhom stopped. He dug a hole and took a drink of water. Then he turned to the left and went on.

By now Pakhom was very tired. He looked at the sun and saw that it was noon. "I must stop and rest," he said.

Pakhom sat down on the ground. He ate some bread and drank

some water. Then he went on again. The food made him feel better. But he was very hot. He also felt sleepy.

Pakhom walked for a long time. He was going to turn to the left. But he looked at the land ahead of him. It was very good land. "I must have that piece of land," he thought. So he walked on.

Pakhom went about a mile. Then he dug a hole and turned to the left. Now he looked toward the hill. It seemed very, very far away. It was so far away that it was hard for him to see it. He looked at the sun. It was just beginning to set.

Pakhom thought, "I must hurry back **right now**! I must go back at once! Perhaps I went too far! Anyhow, I have a big piece of land."

Pakhom headed toward the hill, but it was hard to walk. His feet were cut and his legs felt weak. He wanted to rest, but that was not possible. He *had* to get back before the sun set! And the sun was going down.

"Oh, dear," thought Pakhom, "did I go too far? Can I get back in time? What if I am too late?"

Pakhom looked at the hill. Then he looked at the sun. He was still far from the hill—and the sun was almost down!

It was very hard to walk, but he went faster and faster. He hurried on. But he was still far from the hill.

Pakhom began to run. He threw away the water and the bread, but he kept the shovel. He **leaned** against it while he ran.

"What shall I do?" he thought. "I was **greedy** and went too far. What if I can't get back before the sun sets?"

His mouth was very dry. And now his heart was beating like a hammer. It was pounding very loudly. Still he went on. He could not stop.

"I can't stop now!" he thought. "They will call me a fool if I stop now! I have run very far. I can't stop now!"

He ran on and on. Then he heard the Bashkirs. They were yelling at him. They were cheering. They were shouting at him to keep running. Pakhom heard them. He kept running.

The sun was almost down. Yes, the sun was about to set. It was very low in the sky. But Pakhom was very near the hill! He could see the people on the hill! They were waving their arms at him. They were shouting at him to hurry.

Pakhom could see the spot where he started. He could see the fur hat on the ground. He could see the rubles on the hat. And he could see the Chief! The Chief was sitting on the ground. He seemed to be smiling. Then Pakhom remembered his dream. He wondered if he would get the land.

Pakhom looked at the sun. It was almost down! It was nearly touching the ground! He rushed on.

Just as he reached the hill, it suddenly got dark. Pakhom looked up. He saw that the sun had set! He cried out, "I have lost everything!"

Pakhom stopped running. But then he heard the Bashkirs. They were still shouting. They were yelling at him to hurry. Then Pakhom remembered that they were *on top* of the hill. He was at the bottom. They could still see the sun!

He took a deep breath and ran up the hill. It was still light there! Pakhom reached the top. He saw the fur hat! He saw the Chief! The Chief was still smiling. Again Pakhom remembered his dream.

Pakhom cried out, "*Ahhhh*!" As he fell forward, his fingers touched the hat.

"Well done!" cried the Chief. "Much land is yours!"

Pakhom's helper ran to him. He tried to help Pakhom get up. But Pakhom did not move. Blood was flowing from his mouth. Pakhom was dead!

The Bashkirs shook their heads sadly.

The helper took the shovel and dug a **grave.** A little piece of land was all that he needed. It was just big enough for Pakhom to lie in. It was six feet long from his head to his toes.

YOU CAN ANSWER THESE QUESTIONS

Put an *x* in the box next to the correct answer.

Reading Comprehension

1. Pakhom began to walk toward the
- ❏ **a.** west.
- ❏ **b.** east.
- ❏ **c.** south.

2. As Pakhom walked along, he
- ❏ **a.** dug holes.
- ❏ **b.** sang songs.
- ❏ **c.** shouted at the Bashkirs.

3. Pakhom threw away
- ❏ **a.** the shovel.
- ❏ **b.** the water and the bread.
- ❏ **c.** his belt.

4. It was hard for Pakhom to walk because
- ❏ **a.** the land was covered with rocks.
- ❏ **b.** he didn't know where he was going.
- ❏ **c.** his feet were cut and his legs felt weak.

5. Pakhom began to hurry back when he
- ❏ **a.** looked at his watch and saw that it was late.
- ❏ **b.** heard the Chief calling him.
- ❏ **c.** saw that the sun was beginning to set.

6. Pakhom thought the Chief was
- ❏ **a.** smiling.
- ❏ **b.** crying.
- ❏ **c.** shaking his head sadly.

Vocabulary

7. As he ran, Pakhom leaned against the shovel. The word *leaned* means
- ❏ **a.** rested against.
- ❏ **b.** yelled at.
- ❏ **c.** broke into pieces.

8. Pakhom said, "I was greedy and went too far." Someone who is *greedy*
- ❏ **a.** wants very little.
- ❏ **b.** wants too much.
- ❏ **c.** gives things away.

9. The helper dug a grave for Pakhom. A *grave* is a
- ❏ **a.** small wooden box.
- ❏ **b.** small garden.
- ❏ **c.** hole in the ground for a dead body.

Idioms

10. When it got late Pakhom said, "I must hurry back right now!" The idiom *right now* means
- ❏ **a.** at once.
- ❏ **b.** in an hour.
- ❏ **c.** later.

How many questions did you answer correctly? Circle your score. Then fill in your score on the Score Chart on page 168.

Number Correct	1	2	3	4	5	6	7	8	9	10
Score	10	20	30	40	50	60	70	80	90	100

EXERCISES TO HELP YOU

Exercise A

Understanding the story. Answer each question by writing a complete sentence. Begin each sentence with a capital letter. End each sentence with a period. You may use the line numbers in parentheses to find the answers.

1. Which way did Pakhom walk? (3)

_____

2. Why did Pakhom take off his boots? (19)

_____

3. Why did Pakhom have to hurry back? (46)

_____

4. Why was it hard for him to walk? (52)

_____

5. What did Pakhom throw away? (61)

_____

6. What were the Bashkirs shouting at Pakhom? (71)

_____

7. When he saw the Chief smiling, what did Pakhom remember? (80)

_____

8. After Pakhom fell, why didn't he move? (98)

_____

9. What did the helper dig? (101)

_____

10. How big was Pakhom's grave? (103)

_____

Exercise B

Building sentences. Make sentences by adding the correct letter. Each sentence tells something about in the story.

1. _____ Pakhom carried the shovel over		**a.** was beginning to set.
2. _____ He walked for a mile and		**b.** his shoulder.
3. _____ Pakhom turned and looked back		**c.** looked very small.
4. _____ The people on the hill		**d.** then dug the first hole.
5. _____ Pakhom saw that the sun		**e.** toward the hill.

Now write the sentences on the lines below. Remember to begin each sentence with a capital letter and to end each sentence with a period.

1. _____

2. _____

3. _____

4. _____

5. _____

Now do questions 6–10 the same way.

6. _____ Pakhom began to		**a.** yelling at him to hurry.
7. _____ His heart was beating		**b.** run back to the hill.
8. _____ He heard the Bashkirs		**c.** touched the hat.
9. _____ Finally his fingers		**d.** he was dead.
10. _____ Pakhom did not move because		**e.** very loudly.

6. _____

7. _____

8. _____

_____

9. _____

10. _____

Exercise C

Adding vocabulary. On the left are 8 words from the story. Complete each sentence by adding the correct word.

marched

direction

boots

flowing

pile

waving

rise

possible

1. Pakhom turned to the east and waited for the sun to _____.

2. He walked down the hill and _____ on to the plain.

3. He put the little _____ of earth next to the hole.

4. His heavy _____ made it hard to walk.

5. Pakhom said, "I have gone far enough in this _____."

6. The Bashkirs were _____ their arms at him.

7. Pakhom wanted to rest but that was not _____.

8. Blood was _____ from his mouth.

Exercise D

Writing verbs correctly. Fill in each blank by writing *Present*, *Past*, or *Future* to show the tense of the verb in each sentence. The first one has been done for you.

1. Pakhom looked around. ___*Past*___

2. The land was very good. _____

3. I will walk to the east. _____

4. Pakhom dug another hole. _____

5. He sits on the ground. _____

6. I am very tired. _____

7. I will have a large piece of land. _____

8. He will sell some of the land. _____

9. They are on top of the hill. _____

10. Pakhom went too far. _____

11. They will call me a fool. _____

12. The hill is far away. _____

13. He sees the fur hat. _____

14. Pakhom fell to the ground. _____

15. The Bashkirs were sad. _____

Exercise E

Changing statements to questions. Change each statement to a question. Begin each question with the word or words in parentheses. Put a question mark at the end of each question. The first one has been done for you.

1. Pakhom saw the hill. (What)

   What did Pakhom see?

2. The food made him feel better. (What)

   _____

3. His heart was beating loudly. (How)

   _____

4. Pakhom walked for three miles. (How far)

   _____

5. Pakhom ate some bread. (What)

   _____

6. Pakhom was very near the hill. (Where)

   _____

7. Pakhom saw the Chief. (Who)

   _____

8. Pakhom remembered his dream. (What)

   _____

9. They could see the sun because they were on top of the hill. (Why)

   _____

10. A little piece of land was all that the helper needed. (How much)

    _____

Exercise F

Vocabulary review. Write a complete sentence for each word or group of words.

1. boots _____

_____

2. rise _____

_____

3. pile _____

_____

4. marched _____

_____

5. direction _____

_____

6. waving _____

_____

7. flowing _____

_____

8. possible _____

_____

9. leaned _____

_____

10. greedy _____

_____

11. grave _____

_____

12. right now _____

_____

SHARING WITH OTHERS

It is fun to share ideas with others. Discuss these questions with your partner or with the group. Write your answer to one of the questions.

◆ What killed Pakhom? Explain your answer.
◆ At the end of the story, how big was the piece of land that Pakhom got? What do you think this means?

_____

_____

_____

_____

_____

_____

_____

Irregular Verbs

Verb	Past Tense	Past Participle	Verb	Past Tense	Past Participle
be (am/is/are)	was/were	been	leave	left	left
become	became	become	lie	lay	lain
begin	began	begun	lose	lost	lost
bring	brought	brought	make	made	made
build	built	built	put	put	put
buy	bought	bought	ride	rode	ridden
catch	caught	caught	run	ran	run
cut	cut	cut	say	said	said
come	came	come	see	saw	seen
die	died	died	sell	sold	sold
do	did	done	send	sent	sent
drive	drove	driven	set	set	set
eat	ate	eaten	shake	shook	shaken
fall	fell	fallen	sit	sat	sat
find	found	found	sleep	slept	slept
fly	flew	flown	speak	spoke	spoken
get	got	gotten	spend	spent	spent
give	gave	given	steal	stole	stolen
go	went	gone	strike	struck	struck
grow	grew	grown	take	took	taken
have	had	had	teach	taught	taught
hear	heard	heard	tell	told	told
hold	held	held	think	thought	thought
keep	kept	kept	throw	threw	thrown
know	knew	known			

Score Chart

This is the Score Chart for You can answer these questions. Shade in your score for each part of the story. For example, if your score was 80 for Part 1 of **Wolf**, look at the bottom of the chart for Part 1, **Wolf**. Shade in the bar up to the 80 mark. By looking at this chart, you can see how well you did on each part of the story.

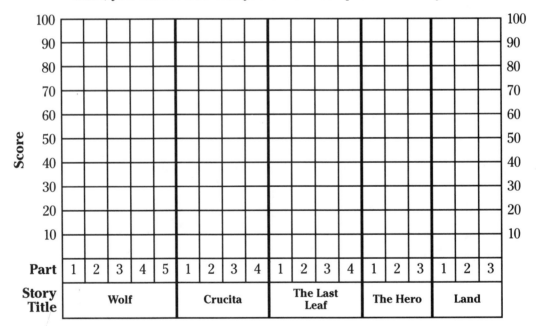

Score																			
100																			
90																			
80																			
70																			
60																			
50																			
40																			
30																			
20																			
10																			
Part	1	2	3	4	5	1	2	3	4	1	2	3	4	1	2	3	1	2	3
Story Title	Wolf					Crucita				The Last Leaf				The Hero			Land		